21St Century Organizations

How to Meet the 21St Century Skills Gap

ISBN-13: 978-1502974983

ISBN-10: 1502974983

Copyright © 2014 by Roxanne Sawatzky

All rights reserved

Cover design: Jelena Gajic

Printed in the United States of America by CreateSpace

Bulk purchases, please contact empoweringchange@mymts.net

Website: empoweringchange.ca

Without limiting the rights under the copyright reserved above, no part of this publication may be reproduced, stored in or introduced into a retrieval system, or transmitted in any form or by any means (electronic, mechanical, by photocopying, recording or otherwise) without the prior written permission of the copyright owner and the publisher of the book.

The scanning, uploading, and distribution of this book via the Internet or by any other means without the permission of the author is illegal and punishable by law. Please purchase only authorized printed or electronic editions and do not participate in or encourage electronic piracy of copyrighted materials.

Your support of the author's rights is appreciated.

George you made this book and all my projects possible, for this I thank you.

Table of Contents

Introduction 1

Chapter 1: A Brief History of Industry in the Modern Era 3
    19th Century 4
    20th Century and the Skills Gap 6
    21st Century 9

Chapter 2: 21st Century Characteristics 11
    Innovation 11
    Adaptability is Crucial in the Modern-Day Organization 15
    Flexibility is Adaptability's Next of Kin 17
    Emotional Intelligence in the 21st Century Workplace 19
    Ever-Changing Technology in the 21st Century Organization .. 22
    Systems Thinking 25

Chapter 3: The Dilemma of the Skills Gap 29
    Why Organizations Are Not Having Their Needs Met 30
    An Organization Defined and the Skills Gap 33

Chapter 4: Tools for Bridging the Skills Gap 40
    Education in the 21st Century 41
    Globalization is a Must 44

Chapter 5: The 21st Century Approach to Innovation 48
    Innovation Wasn't Always Welcomed 48
    The Organization of the 21st Century Must Foster Innovation .. 51
        Create a workplace that is innovative by cultivating an
            environment of problem solving 54
        Create a happy place 56
        Encourage a healthy lifestyle 56

Chapter 6: Leadership in the 21st Century 59
    Traditional Leadership 59
    Leadership in a 21st Century Organization 61
        Transactional leadership: A thing of the past? 61

    Transformational leadership: The wave of the future............62
    Bureaucratic leadership vs. charismatic leadership 63
    Horizontal leadership vs, vertical leadership 64
        Horizontal leadership saves time 64
        Horizontal leadership boosts morale 64
        Horizontal leadership facilitates innovation 65
    The concept of servant leadership..65
    Parallels between leadership types and styles.......................66
Characteristics of an Effective 21st Century Leader 67
    Lead by example 67
    Be open-minded 67
    Communicate well 68
    Embrace technology..68
    Be willing to sacrifice for the greater good 69

Chapter 7: Staying Relevant in the Age of Knowledge 70
    Everyone is a Learner 71
    Harnessing Intellectual Capital 72
    Change Will Come—Embrace it and Facilitate it! 73
    Communication is Crucial 75
    Technology Changes Rapidly, and We Must Adapt................76
    With Diversity Comes Growth 77

Conclusion 80

References..83

Introduction

"Progress is impossible without change, and those who cannot change their minds cannot change anything." ~ *George Bernard Shaw*

You, like many others, have heard that in today's world, the only constant is change. Given this truth, I would invite you to consider for a moment constant change within the following context. With new technologies being released daily to the general public, we hear announcements proclaiming innovative ways to communicate and glean information, and of course we are reminded that there are innovative ways to conduct business. It can feel overwhelming to keep up, let alone lead the way in this current global culture, which is also deemed the *Knowledge Age*. You may be asking, "What can an organization do to stay ahead of the curve in a world that is being remodeled on a minute-by-minute basis?" Within this book, I will discuss that and more.

In Chapter 1, I begin with a trip down memory lane, where the historic foundations that shape our modern-day organizations will be explored, including the dilemmas they face in terms of maintaining their relevance in a world that is future-focused.

In Chapter 2, I describe key characteristics an organization will need in order to not only keep up with the demands of today's world, but to do so while cultivating a culture of ideas and innovation that will propel them into the future. It is not enough, however, to know what these characteristics are; I will also discuss ways and means for organizations seeking a road map to develop or enhance their current approaches.

Next, in Chapters 3 and 4, I will identify and explore skills gaps: what they are, how they can and do affect your business, and how to bridge them effectively in your organization.

In Chapter 5, I will discuss the 21st century approach to innovation. Specifically, how making changes, introducing new ways of thinking and new methods of operation will impact those businesses and organizations that use the characteristics I speak of in Chapter 2 to embrace a global worldview and economy, while keeping their identity, values, and guiding principles.

Leadership as we knew it is changing. In Chapter 6, I will discuss what leadership in the 21st century may look like and how becoming such a leader will impact each organization, business, and person in real and lasting ways.

Finally, in Chapter 7, I will address the importance of staying relevant in this age of knowledge and advanced technology as well as offering some practical ideas for achieving this goal.

Chapter 1: A Brief History of Industry in the Modern Era

"Your past is important, but as important as it is, it is not nearly as important to your present as the way you see your future." ~ Dr. Tony Campolo

Before I begin exploring what a business requires to thrive in today's world, let's take a moment to explore the foundation upon which the 21st century organization has been built. As with all things new and modern, the organization of today has its roots in the past. Thus, I begin this book on modern-day organizational success with a short history lesson.

The past few centuries have brought much in the way of change, and with great advancements in technology came major changes in the workplace. The rapid rise of technology—automation in particular—was a key factor that brought about the rise of a more urbanized, industrial workforce.

While the 18th century workplace was characterized by intensive manual labour with little yield, the 19th century brought a massive wave of technological development, enabling factories and processing plants to open for business and thrive. The 18th century introduced us to the Industrial Revolution, workplaces traded their less-efficient, manually operated methods of production for the more efficient automation that came about as more and more machines came to be used for production. Workers were no longer forced to toil manually, only to have little output to show for their efforts. With the advent of steam-powered machinery and an increasing move toward industrializing the workforce, workers could now press a few levers and have their work output increased—sometimes a hundredfold or more—without having to break their backs to do it.

Textile manufacturing replaced time-consuming hand-loom weaving, and automatic printing presses took the place of manually operated presses, making publishing a breeze. Agricultural processes that had once required manual labour were now being replaced by steam-driven machinery that caused a sharp increase in farming productivity. Mining for coal and ore became far more productive now that steam engines could aid in draining shafts of excess water; as a result, workers could mine more deeply than they had ever been able to in prior generations. Metal working and chemical production saw great increases during this time, and as more processes came to be streamlined and automated by use of a machine, more businesses thrived. Those businesses that took advantage of the new technology saw their profits boom, and capitalism was on the rise in the Western world.

This Industrial Revolution, along with the dramatic shift away from the old, manual way of doing things and toward the mechanized, automated way of doing things, is at the root of one of the most noteworthy cultural shifts in the history of time—a shift that eventually spread out on a global scale. When workplaces change, so, too, do the cultures in which those workplaces exist. When the 19th century made her grand entrance, significant changes had been made to both workforce and economy—and there were even bigger changes on the horizon waiting to happen.

19th Century

The Industrial Revolution had changed the face of the Western world, and it was in full force during the 19th century. Agricultural businesses flourished, they now had the machinery they needed to increase production beyond the subsistence level. The 19th century saw a huge spike in the use of fossil fuels, such as coal, natural gas, and petroleum. These fossil fuels were used as an efficient energy source that replaced the less-efficient means used in the past: Kerosene could light lamps and heat homes, and coal could be burned in its raw form—without the need for further refinement or processing—to create heat energy needed to propel steam-powered machinery.

By the mid-19th century, internal combustion engines, which ran on fossil fuels, again changed the face of the world—and the face of industry. If the shift caused by the beginnings of the Industrial Revolution in the 18th century had been great, the shift caused by the rise of the internal combustion engine in the 19th century and into the 20th century was gargantuan—for the internal combustion engine was the crux that allowed for the mass-production of automobiles.

Let's pause for a moment, though, to reflect upon what these big changes in industry meant for business leaders, managers, and employees. In the 19th century, with the rise of industry and mass production and factory work, came certain norms in the culture of the workplace. Managers now had more employees than ever, and there was a distinctive divide between those in power and those who were beneath them.

Managers were pressured by leaders to train as many mass production labourers and trades people as possible in the shortest amount of time feasible. In turn, managers had their employees on a tight leash, and employees were given little say in the workplace—from working conditions to pay, they were essentially forced to take what they were given, without having a voice with which to speak up for themselves. If someone worked in a factory line and demanded fewer working hours or higher pay, he or she could be fired without any cause and easily replaced by another worker willing to take what he or she was given without inciting any unrest. Labour unions had not yet become a strong force at this point in time, so there were few places for a disgruntled or mistreated factory worker to turn with his or her complaints.

The education system of this era reflected the work culture, which in turn reflected the industrial culture that had overtaken the Western world. Educators were to train students to become good workers—to become quiet and docile cogs in the metaphorical factory machine. Rather than focusing on philosophy or the arts, public education in the 19th century emphasized the importance of things that would be needed when the student later joined the workforce, including the way to behave. Students were rewarded for rote memorization over critical thinking and for adhering strictly to rules that encouraged following instructions versus free thinking. This enabled them to become more suited for the uniformity and standardization that was necessary under the 19th century workforce model.

Sadly, although the many technological advances caused sweeping changes—certainly there were many positive changes for businesses—these changes did little to improve the quality of life for the masses. Workers were not treated as valuable, labour unions did not exist; employees had no place in the workforce to voice their work concerns. Work might prove perilous to life or limb, and there was no expectation of (much less guarantee of) reparation for those who were injured on the job. Employees themselves had little to no bargaining power. The education system was focused on creating a malleable workforce for the production floor rather than being focused on creating college-bound future leaders, and life expectancy was quite low, at around 50 years of age in the 19th century.

20th Century and the Skills Gap

As stated previously, the development and production of the internal combustion engine was to the 20th century what the steam engine had been to the two previous centuries; it was a revolutionary, world-changing development that vastly changed the way business was conducted. The combustion engine made the development and production of motorboats, motorized tractors and other farm equipment, and—perhaps most importantly of all—automobiles possible.

Productivity of agricultural-based businesses increased even more now that equipment powered by internal combustion had become available to them. Manufacturers had newer, more efficient machines to help streamline and even automate mass production on factory floors, and people could now buy automobiles for personal use, although in the early 20th century, the average person could not afford to purchase a car. By the 1930's, the horse and buggy became a relic of the past, and roads were being paved over to make way for auto travel. As cars became more reliable and more copious in number, they became more affordable, and soon many families had an automobile.

The 20th century also saw the invention of the jet airplane and, soon thereafter, the rise of commercial air travel. By the 1950's and 1960's, people could travel in relative safety from one end of the world to the other in less than a day via a commercial airliner—something that in prior centuries would have taken weeks or months by sea and might be at the cost of one's health and well-being.

The technological advancements of the 20th century were rapid-fire; no other period in time had ever seen such swift technological evolution. As soon as something was invented, it was improved upon, rendering the prior model obsolete. When computers were first created, they took up a large room. However, by the end of the 20th century, all the power of that original room-sized computer (and then some!) could fit into the palm of your hand.

All these technological advancements called for people who were experts in how the new and complex technologies functioned, creating a demand for myriad new skill sets that had previously not been needed in the 18th or 19th centuries. With technology on the rise and becoming an ever-present facet of the ever-changing modern world in both business and leisure aspects of life, from personal computer to portable music player, more and more people who knew how to *use* the technology were necessary.

So much was changing in the 20th century. Life as we knew it would never be the same. However, in spite of the many and vast changes taking place during this time period, there were an equal number of things that remained the same. History, in some instances, continued to repeat itself, particularly with regard to how business was conducted.

Although technological advancements led to advancements in industry and medicine, thus allowing people to live longer (to age 65-70 and beyond), as well as the rise of well-organized and empowered labour unions that allowed workers to have the bargaining power they so desperately needed, there were many ways in which organizations remained the same. In fact, many continued to mirror the 19th century, conducting *business as usual* rather than changing with the times. Although workers now had more bargaining power than their 19th century counterparts and were living longer than ever, education practices still remained rooted in practices dictated by 19th century logic that called for docile factory workers rather than critically thinking leaders—whether positional leaders or not. Managers in the 20th century often followed the management model proposed by Frederick Winslow Taylor, the engineer who penned handbooks for managers on improving efficiency with regards to industry.

Although Taylor was quite a pioneer with regard to creating management standards for a modern-day business, his approach had limits and seemed to place low value on employee morale. In essence, his system focused solely on the bottom line without taking into consideration the *human factors* that could improve organizations in such ways as reducing employee turnover or improving efficiency through rewarding employees and, thus, making them *want* to come to work and perform their jobs well. Taylor's management model, although well-intended, served to thicken the line between management and staff, creating an environment of micromanagement on the part of management and leadership and alienation and a sense of devaluation on the part of the labourers. Taylor's model did not lend itself well to the need for a problem-solving, highly skilled workforce with the capacity to evaluate tasks or processes from multiple angles. Rather, it solidified the Industrial Revolution-era management style that called for "keeping workers in their place."

In an era of industry calling for more and more skill and less routine, menial work, Taylor's model of management had become obsolete, and yet, it was and is still being used by organizations everywhere. The public schooling system's curricula remained stuck in the past as well, using an outdated education model and trying to find a way to fit the new material needed to survive in the modern, technologically advanced workplace into traditional teaching practices. These practices proved detrimental to the needs of the ever-changing modern business world, as it created a *skills gap*: the gap between the need for a highly skilled and specialized workforce and the availability of employees with those sought-after skills. Unfortunately, the skills gap continues to be a problem faced by many organizations even in the 21st century.

21st Century

Now we come to our era—the 21st century. Unfortunately, many of the problems faced by 20th century organizations remain issues for 21st century organizations, as well. This is due to adherence to non-operational ways of thinking and outdated ways of conducting business. Many organizations continue to apply Taylor's guidelines when it comes to managing employees, and many schools are still outlining curricula for their students using a 19th century approach. These methodologies do a huge disservice to not only the employees and students, but to the businesses and schools as well—for they are using tactics that could eventually lead to their downfall in the modern world.

The 21st century is a new era, and in light of how cultural, educational, and workplace norms from the past have failed in the face of the rapid advances that typify this era, there is clearly a call for new norms: norms that will help organizations survive and thrive in this exciting time. There is a call for revolution with how we approach education, the workplace, and manager-employee relationships. Using 19th century management tactics has led to a disgruntled workforce and a skills gap, neither of which can serve an organization in any sort of positive capacity. Thus, the 21st century calls for organizations to use a brand new set of business strategies and a new set of cultural, educational, and workplace standards. In order to ride the wave of the future, it is necessary to evolve and, in so doing, leave the ineffective methods behind in favour of a fresh, innovative approach.

"You can and should create your own future; because if you don't, someone else surely will." ~ *Joel Barker*

Chapter 2: 21st Century Characteristics

"The first step toward change is awareness, the second step is acceptance." ~ Nathaniel Branden

The distinguishing characteristics that are common to most profitable businesses, both historically and currently, are unchanging core standards, including effective leadership, commitment to excellence, confidence in their ability to meet and even surpass the needs of their stakeholders, and passion for their purpose. Along with these core characteristics, there are definite 21st century characteristics and defining traits of an organization that is willing and able to not only meet, but also exceed 21st century expectations. Without these characteristics and traits, organizations will find themselves left behind as the world moves to a more global economy and mindset.

There are six key characteristics that the 21st century embodies: innovation, adaptability, flexibility, emotional intelligence, technology, and a *systems thinking* approach. As you will see in this chapter, there will be obvious benefits to embracing these characteristics, and there will be observable disadvantages to those organizations that resist developing these characteristics. As I discuss these characteristics and traits, I will look at how an organization will be impacted both positively and negatively depending on their assimilation of them.

Innovation

Innovation is defined as a new idea, device, or method or the act of introducing these things. These three are interdependent and thrive on one another.

Innovation is happening every day as technological advances continue at a rapid-fire pace. Organizations, businesses, and leaders must possess the spirit of innovation in order to not only be successful and prosperous, but also to survive. As organizations begin to recognize the need for innovation and the introduction of ideas, methods, and systems, leadership will also need to view their workforce through a new lens of understanding and respect. The organization as a whole will require an understanding of the inevitability of change, along with the ability to be flexible and adaptable in managing those changes. This will be key components to the achievement of goals in the 21st century organization.

In considering organizational innovation, it is necessary to step back a moment and point our camera lens towards education, which is a key contributor to the future of our organizations. Bernie Trilling and Charles Fadel (2009) are pioneers in the movement toward 21st century education. Their ideas for revamping the public educations systems are applicable to today's workplace:

> Working their way toward a 21st century model of teaching and learning, the answer for educators and policymakers lies in incorporating both a systematic approach and a spirit of innovation. They need to take both small, achievable steps and some large leaps in the many components of the education system and to measure progress as they go, course correcting as they learn what works and what doesn't and celebrating their accomplishments along the way. (p. 121)

As educators shift to 21st century approaches, they prepare their students, your future employees, with the ability to adapt in an ever-changing workplace. Most importantly, they encourage students to develop their ability to apply a systems thinking mindset, which is integral to an organization's future. Today's leaders and employees can benefit from Trilling and Fadel's (2009) ideas about education. Just as educators make the shift, so too must the organizations, thereby modelling what students have learned in the classroom and expect outside of the schoolroom. Gone are the old days when employees *shut up and showed up*. In order to attract the innovators and keep them, leaders must construct and cultivate an environment that fosters creativity, rewards ideas, and allows for trying *and failing*—an important, but often neglected, component to innovation. Mirroring the 21st century education framework, an organization must also know how to take a moment to pause (without losing momentum) and consider what is working and what is not. There is a fine dance that effective 21st century organizations must emulate.

In order for an organization to remain innovative, they must be committed to learning. Learning organizations create a culture that encourages and supports continuous employee learning, critical thinking, and risk taking with new ideas. They value workplace contributions; they know when to pause and reflect; and they know when to move forward and disseminate the new knowledge throughout the organization for incorporation into day-to-day activities.

An effective organization uses *feedback loops*. Feedback loops take the system output into consideration, which enables the organization to adjust its performance to meet a desired outcome. Feedback loops permit organizations to innovate, allowing them to consistently provide new and better services that directly address their stakeholders. While many organizations recognize the need to be innovative, unfortunately, many seem to point their lens in the wrong direction. Feedback loops encourage organizations to look at their stakeholders and tap into what they want. Input from the stakeholders allows for self-correction of a method, process, or service. While an organization may recognize the importance of feedback loops, they must also put a system in place for people to provide feedback.

Effective 21st century organizations are able to determine what lens they need for various situations. Essentially, they know how to use multiple lenses; they can soar in a helicopter so to speak, giving them the ability to look down and see the vastness of the organization and potential for innovation. They can also shift their lens and view the organization from a balcony level, thereby coming in for a closer look, allowing for reflection and evaluation. They can also zoom right in and view the organization from the ground level, thereby taking inventory of what is not working and making the necessary adjustments after reflecting on their balcony view. This ability to smoothly transition their lens to view the system is an essential characteristic of an innovative 21st century organization.

While innovation is at the forefront of a leader's mind, a truly innovative organization recognizes that it must create a space for failure in order to reach innovation. In doing so, leaders motivate and even inspire employees to be learners and result in successful businesses. While many businesses are reluctant to let go of their current business model entirely, and wisely so, small but consistent changes in policy and procedures and big changes in attitude will begin to create the essential 21st century characteristic of *adaptability*.

Remember that not everything needs to change all at once. The process of modeling a 21st century mindset can be made by taking *one-degree shifts*. Imagine a compass, if you're driving in one direction and then make a one-degree shift, eventually, if you drive far enough, you will end up in a very different place. One organization I recently worked with decided they would begin with each department taking a one-degree shift. As a result, the organization ended with 15 one-degree shifts. The change was imperceptible at first, but over time, it highlighted the collective significance of these individual shifts.

Adaptability is Crucial in the Modern-Day Organization

While the ability to innovate is critical, so is the capability to respond quickly to opportunities and make changes within the workplace. System-wide adaptability is a desperately needed, but rarely seen, characteristic in the 21st century organization. While some departments seem to adapt to change quickly, others lag behind, as a result stalling out the system. The organization will not only need to adapt itself to new products or services or new stakeholders, it also must adapt internally. The desire to remain static and reach equilibrium is enticing for many employees. While finding balance is not a bad thing, it can prevent an organization from being adaptable. The *Merriam-Webster Dictionary* offers the following definition of adaptable: "being able to change or be changed in order to fit or work better in some situation or for some purpose." The definition emphasizes what is required in our current and future workforce.

The *ability* to adapt, though, is not enough. A transformation in attitude toward *change* is needed. According to Herbert C. Kelman of Harvard University, three processes of attitude change are *compliance*, *identification*, and *internalization*. It is important to note that while compliance is necessary, this alone is not the goal for successful adaptation to a new idea or system. Organizations will find that it is necessary to integrate changes in both big and small ways in order to ensure the internalization of new ideas, which is a key factor in a lasting change in attitude.

There was a time when company owners and business leaders were less concerned with an employee's attitude and more concerned with his or her behaviour. While a compliant employee may look good to the untrained eye, it is important to realize that anyone can be forced to comply outwardly, but an employee who has an internal struggle with management or policy will show his or her hand in a number of ways, not the least of which is resistance to change and pollution of the work environment. A toxic culture may go unnoticed to leadership, but be aware that staff and employees are likely feeling the effects of the negative environment. People without power will leverage what they can, and while it may *appear* that they are adapting, they may in fact be stalling out any real progress within the department. This is often happening without leadership knowledge, while not always the case, workplace culture has a way of keeping the inner dynamics out of the eye of leadership. Leadership can address this dilemma by conducting periodic anonymous surveys asking staff to share their observations and put forth what they need to successfully adapt to change.

Attitude is paramount in importance when considering an organization that can adapt quickly, because "one bad apple spoils the whole barrel." A disgruntled employee or, worse, a leader with a negative attitude can change the atmosphere of a workplace in a matter of moments, and over time, this environment may lead to stress-related violence, accidents, illnesses, and absences. Further, poor attitudes among the workforce and leadership of a company can and will stifle creativity, productivity, and loss of profits. A negative attitude can also damage that necessary edge that non-profits require to keep their funding.

In order to stay current in this constantly changing world of technological advances that are and will always be present in a 21st century organization, we must be adaptable in our attitudes, mindsets, and businesses practices. It will not be enough to be *open-minded* and considerate towards change, but instead, it is and will continue to be necessary to assess an idea or instrument and determine its usefulness and necessity in our own company or life and, based on that assessment, to quickly adapt and implement this new approach.

I would challenge organizations to not only learn to be adaptable, but to also build competency in this area. By doing so, the organization can continuously introduce change while seeing low resistance to ongoing change. The challenge for leadership is finding that delicate line where they nudge employees out of the comfort zone and into the learning zone without crossing into the anxiety zone. When staff members are in the comfort zone, they become bored and the status quo becomes the norm. In the learning zone, staff are adapting to new approaches. Finally, in the anxiety zone, people shut down, and this is where we see the flight/flight response. If employees are pushed into this place, learning, innovation, and adaptability are lost.

Individuals will need to demonstrate the ability to quickly but thoughtfully learn a new objective, process, or model, which will allow for necessary organizational change. In order to stay relevant even in the face of opposition, an organization will need to demonstrate the competency of adaptability. Not everyone is gifted with a natural capacity for adaptability, but it can be learned progressively with practice.

Flexibility is Adaptability's Next of Kin

Flexibility is another characteristic requisite of the 21st century business model. While adaptability is being able to change, *flexibility* is being willing to change. Without willingness, ability is not an issue. For example, a child may be physically able to eat his broccoli at dinnertime, but if he isn't willing, that broccoli will still be there at the end of the meal unless some force or coercion is applied. Since force and coercion are not advantageous in the workplace, or anywhere else really, then willingness is key to success.

Flexibility will be required on the part of leaders, managers, employees, stakeholders, and owners alike. If one part of the whole is unwilling to adapt to the changes necessary to create more current and proactive business practices, success is tenuous at best.

Like adaptability, flexibility can be accomplished through consistent practice. Consider the body as an example:

> When a sedentary person decides it is time to become more healthy and strong, he will likely begin a fitness routine. Any solid fitness routine will begin with stretching the muscles to avoid injury. When a normally sedentary person begins to add physical exercise to their lifestyle, their flexibility is limited due to the underuse of the muscle. However, with repeated training, consistent stretching and use of the muscles, their range of motion and flexibility will increase, often substantially.

Some ways to *model the way* and exercise your flexibility muscles as an leader might be to create days that benefit your employees personally, such as *casual Friday* where the typical business attire is relaxed a bit, flexible scheduling that allows for some to arrive and/or leave earlier or later depending on their personal needs, or maybe offer the president's parking space to an outstanding employee one day a week or month—anything that will let your people know that you are modelling the way. Continue to consider new ways of doing things, which will result in others demonstrating flexibility, which soon leads to flexibility in action.

After you have successfully initiated flexibility through your own actions as a leader, you can then expect your workforce to consider some new ways of doing things, new ideas, or new practices. The change you want to see really begins with leaders, I would encourage you to begin with compassion, listen to, and consider the feedback your employees give. The benefit will be two-fold: first, they will begin to trust that they matter to you and your organization, and next, they will be more willing to comply with and embrace changes.

Emotional Intelligence in the 21st Century Workplace

According to Plato, "all learning has an emotional base." Learning is critical in this ever changing world, and while emotion has taken a back seat to intelligence in business historically, it is becoming increasingly obvious that *emotional intelligence*, or the "ability to perceive, control, and evaluate emotions", is critical to a positive and functional work environment. For example, in a recent survey conducted for Careerbuilder by Harris Interactive (2011), it was found that "seventy-one percent [of hiring managers] said they value emotional intelligence in an employee more than IQ" (para. 1). Survey respondents felt that persons with a higher emotional intelligence are more likely to stay calm and react proactively during stressful situations and are further more likely to help others, be open to critique, and learn from their mistakes. The changing perception of the value of emotional intelligence in the workplace reflects the changes that organizations have undergone as they merge into the Knowledge Age. After all, emotional intelligence is a form of knowledge too.

Peter Salovey and John D. Mayer (1990), leading researchers of and authorities on emotional intelligence define emotional intelligence as "the subset of social intelligence that involves the ability to monitor one's own and others' feelings and emotions, to discriminate among them and to use this information to guide one's thinking and actions" (p. 189). For some people it is quite natural to pick up the "energy" in the room. While for others they seem to be completely unaware of an emotional shift in a meeting or office.

Many people have received the message implicitly or explicitly, within their family structure, school, or society, to "suck it up" or "put on a happy face." Many individuals have been raised to shut down their emotions, and for this reason, some individuals not only lack in emotional intelligence, but view emotions as weak or inconsequential. The truth is that everyone experiences a range of emotions, and learning to express our own and perceive another's emotions is critical both personally and within the 21st century organization.

In their 1998 paper, *Bringing Emotional Intelligence to Work*, Cary Cherniss, Daniel Goleman, Robert Emmerling, Kimberly Cowan, and Mitchel Adler noted the following:

> Emotional incompetence often results from habits deeply learned early in life…Connections that are unused become weakened, while those that people use over and over grow increasingly strong. When these habits have been so heavily learned, the underlying neural circuitry becomes the brain's default option at any moment. Thus, for the shy engineer, diffidence is a habit that must be overcome and replaced with a new habit, self-confidence. (p. 5)

So what happens to those who lack important emotional competencies? Cherniss et al. noted "that one must first unlearn old habits and then develop new ones. For the learner, this usually means a long and sometimes difficult process involving much practice" (p. 6) meaning that 1-day seminars are not enough. That said, learning social and emotional intelligence is quite possible with acceptance of new approaches, determination to develop new skills, and a lot of practice.

Emotional intelligence in the workplace creates an atmosphere of acceptance and a culture of concern, and it fosters team participation. When we can be counted on to control our negative emotions while having compassion for others who are experiencing them, we create a place where ideas can be shared without the fear of ridicule. Additionally, while it is important to understand our negative emotions such as disappointment, anger, and dissatisfaction, and be able to read those of others, it is equally important to be able to express and discern positive emotions such as delight, acceptance, and contentment. All of these emotions and the awareness of them are critical in not only employee interaction, but also to customer relations and client satisfaction.

Alternatively, when emotions are consistently displaced or overlooked, workers tend to become lethargic at least and disgruntled or even violent in the worst cases. The inability to *read* a customer, client, or situation creates further scenarios where employees are put in harm's way simply by not having this skill set to perceive and address circumstances when they arise.

Those who have lower emotional intelligence, who don't acknowledge their feelings, evaluate their emotions critically, and control their emotions in a positive way are more likely to carry out acts of aggression towards others, ranging from verbal insults and bullying to sabotage and physical violence. The Occupational Safety and Health Administration of the United States Department of Labour (2014) lists "working with volatile, unstable people" (para. 2) as a risk factor for workplace violence, and the Centers for Disease Control and Prevention (1996) states that:

> Violence is a substantial contributor to occupational injury and death, and homicide has become the second leading cause of occupational injury death. Each week, an average of 20 workers are murdered and 18,000 are assaulted while at work or on duty. Nonfatal assaults result in millions of lost workdays and cost workers millions of dollars in lost wages. (para. 6)

These instances are the extreme and on the decline according to those same entities; however, any occasion of workplace aggression is detrimental to your employees and to your bottom line. With further education and training, this number will continue to decline. Picking up and discussing the emotional cues given off from colleagues can be a difficult proposition to even the healthiest workplace. A framework that everyone learns and agrees upon will help encourage the growth of this important characteristic.

Father of Lateral Thinking, Edward De Bono, summed it up succinctly in his quote, which said, "Studies have shown that 90% of error in thinking is due to error in perception. If you can change your perception, you can change your emotion and this can lead to new ideas." Successful 21st century businesses will be about change, they will be about perception, and they will be about ideas. Emotional intelligence is a necessary part of this formula and is not to be overlooked by wise leaders.

Ever-Changing Technology in the 21st Century Organization

It simply cannot be overstated: The role of technology in a 21st century organization is paramount.

In its simplest definition, *technology* means "to use science in problem solving." This definition comes directly from a children's dictionary and illustrates that while technology can feel complex and overwhelming, it is something we all use consistently without even thinking about it.

Consider this: Every modern convenience we have that communicates, shares ideas and information, or processes and transacts business uses technology to solve a problem.

For example:

- Our partner is in Singapore, but needs specific information related to our office's floor plan. We use the technological advance of digital information exchange through email, iCloud, fax, or other.

- A patient resides in Toronto, Ontario, but has a heart attack while on vacation in Florence, Italy. Because our office is technologically equipped, we can share the vital information he cannot relay in his current state. Additionally, because he is at a hospital that is also well technologically equipped, he can have the tests and procedures necessary to save his life in the least invasive way possible and that information can be transferred to the necessary offices before he schedules his next appointment.
- Let's bring it closer to home: I'm at work, it is 10:00 am, and I have a meeting at 10:30 am, but the school just called to inform me that my daughter has forgotten her lunch money, again, and they will not be issuing her further credit. Because of the ability to pay online, I can ensure that my daughter's lunch is paid for, and I can still make my meeting. Everyone wins because the school and my bank have utilized technology to address a potential problem, and I have a phone equipped with the modern technological advances to carry out the necessary functions.

The examples are endless, because technology really is everywhere. There are, and always will be, some disadvantages to the advancement of technology. Some hold to the belief that increased technology is causing people to become less active and less personally engaged with other humans. This, of course, can be a problem, and as a business owner or leader of an organization, you may have to address issues such as these. Still, technology will continue to be a part of our lives and, very probably, a bigger part. By and large, change is a choice, and it is not required presently that you embrace technology, but in order to do big business, and especially in order to thrive in a 21st century business environment, you will need to incorporate technology and all the benefits it can offer.

While technology is critical to our future on the planet, the need for technology has come at a cost. Daniel Goleman (2013) posits that "technology captures our attention and disrupts our connections". Furthermore, he states, "Children are growing up in a new reality, one where they are attuning more to machines and less to people than has ever been true in human history" (p. 6). Many organizations today have had to establish rules stating no cell phones, IPad, or laptops will be permitted in meetings in order for people to focus on meeting discussions. I have had to ask for similar considerations while leading my training, while a relatively simply request it is not always easy for participants to let go of technology for a couple of hours. I hold firm that if participants have the their phones close by it is a challenge as their attention is divided and many struggle to be present and contribute to important discussions. The need to be intentional, to have meaningful face-to-face contact, has never been greater, given the advancement of technology in today's world. Daniel Goleman among others speaks of the inability that many of us have to resist checking email, Facebook, and other similar platforms.

This is a valid concern, especially among some age groups, but there is another side to this coin. Technology, in the form of Skype or VOIP platforms, social media, and other such creations, have made it possible for persons with limited mobility, mental or social limitations, or extreme phobias to be able to communicate and engage with others as never before.

Formerly, when a loved one moved away, you would communicate with them by traditional mail, phone, or email. Now, though your friend or loved one is in another country or another state, you can have a face-to-face visit with them by applications such as Facetime, Skype, or other voice and image media. Even if you cannot take a trip to a faraway place, often, you can now watch your grandchildren grow or see the progress as it occurs on a new building in another location.

The issue of technology versus personal interaction has and will remain an issue; however, technology is here to stay and will continue develop. The way to create a balance between one and the other is to make balance a priority. Create functions where your employees get to know one another, such as interdepartmental lunches or dinners; *think tanks* where groups must come together to talk about a current issue your organization is facing but cannot bring their phones, tablets, or laptops with them; or for the really adventurous, consider a company retreat where there are no digital appliances allowed in common places. It takes practice, and to some, the idea of not being *connected* is really frightening. However, with time and patience and planning, human interaction can become and remain balanced in the workplace and among your workforce. You will benefit by having happier, healthier, and more balanced people on your team.

Systems Thinking

The last and one of the most important of the six key characteristics of a 21st century organization is *systems thinking*. Systems thinking is a modern term attributed to Barry Richmond in 1987, which basically means we are all interdependent, that every part of an organization influences and impacts the whole, and how you perceive each part in relation to the whole affects how you manage each task and situation.

Peter Senge (2006), author of *The Fifth Discipline*, systems scientist, and senior lecturer at the MIT Sloan School of Management, explains in his essay how systems' thinking influences an organization:

> As the process of individual visioning unfolds among a group committed to a common endeavour, the underlying purpose and vision of the group begin to emerge…A systemic view of personal power entails empowering the

individual to manifest his or her own personal power simultaneously with empowering the organization to manifest its purpose. The distinction between individual and group blurs in this process, just as happens in the exceptional jazz ensemble or championship sports team. This view implies thinking of the organization as an organism. In this context, system dynamics becomes a way for the organization to know itself better and evolve its design to more effectively accomplish its purpose.

While it may be obvious that in some cases one part of the whole is more *practically* valuable to a process, such as the surgeon's skill seems more valuable than the instrument technician's skills to a patient, systems thinking reminds us that all parts are crucial to the overall health of the organization. However, in the case of the operation, while the surgeon may be the obvious key to a successful surgery, if the instrument tech hasn't done his or her part correctly, infection or other difficulties could ensue.

The practical application to a systems thinking mentality is in leadership. A leader who ignites passion and purpose in his/her nominally intelligent team will be more successful than the leader who has a team of wildly intelligent but uninspired persons. In the 21st century organization, the success of a company will be contingent on the sum of its parts, and this, in essence, is what systems thinking is all about. No one person or department is independent of the other, instead each department understands that they are all interconnected and together they impact the larger system. Daniel Goleman (2013) offers "systems are virtually invisible to the naked eye, but their workings can be rendered visible by gathering data from enough points that the outlines of their dynamics come into focus" (p. 133). Most organizations are explicit about collecting such data and most people will say they understand the basic principle of systems thinking. For example, that *paying it forward* does a good thing to the greater system, most people however, do not really grasp the concept of system thinking as the system as a whole is mostly undetectable therefore not a primary consideration.

Take for example, how machines have now replaced people in some workplaces, how has this change impacted the greater system? For the most part an individual will consider the obvious positive and negatives. A positive the organization can reduce the cost of a product and remain competitive. A negative would be the job loss and the impact that has on a community. That change however, goes far beyond the surface. Looking beyond the surface is systems thinking.

Solving organizational problems requires a system approach, which requires having all stakeholders in the room. Goleman (2013) continues "one of the worst results of system blindness occurs when leaders implement a strategy to solve a problem-but ignore the pertinent system dynamics" (p 142). It is not unusual to see leadership make a decision without inviting the system while it appears more efficient and seamless, this characteristic does not line up with 21st century approaches. Creating a space to hear from the system may take more time on the front end however; it will assist organizations in becoming their best, most-effective selves in order to facilitate a strong and successful organization.

"Everything affects everything else in one way or another. Whether you are aware of that or not does not change the fact that this is what is happening. That's why I say a business is a system. This systems perspective reminds us that this is what is going on. And when you see it this way, you can manage your business better. You appreciate, for example, that any action will reverberate throughout the entire company. This causes you to pay more attention to what you do, and learn the right lessons from your experience." ~ *John Woods, Work in Progress*

While these six key characteristics of innovation, adaptability, flexibility, emotional intelligence, technology, and a systems thinking approach are not the only distinguishing traits of a thriving 21st century organization, in my opinion, they exemplify one. A business that operates according to these ideals will be a leader in its field and a triumph in general.

Chapter 3: The Dilemma of the Skills Gap

"If you don't change direction, you may end up where you are heading." ~ Lau Tzu

In essence, a *skills gap* is the term for the apparent disparity between an employer's need for skilled workers and the workers' available skills.

According to Dennis Yang, president and COO of Udemy in his guest post on *Forbes.com,*

> The disconnect between how educators and employers see college graduates' preparedness provides insight into one source of this problem skills gap. While 72 percent of educational institutions believe recent graduates are ready for work, only 42 percent of employers agree, according to a McKinsey study. (para. 2)

This information sheds light on one of the possible reasons for the skills gap in recent college graduates, but there is another explanation for an organization's skills gap dilemma: the refusal to let go of old ways of running an organization yields a skills gap as well. As I mentioned in Chapter 1, the refusal to let go of old outdated ways of leading or managing an organization yields a skills gap. This gap between what organizations *need* from their employees, in terms of skill, education, and ability, and what their employees (or potential employees) *offer* in terms of those attributes is very often the difference between long-term profitability and catastrophic loss.

Some businesses insist that the skills gap is related to unprepared workers—workers and applicants who either do not possess the skills an organization needs or are unable to adequately perform those skills. Another school of thought is that employers expect potential candidates and employees to already possess all the skills and means necessary to perform their tasks without adequate training, tools, or incentives.

Both of these ideologies are short sighted. The skills gap as it relates to the key characteristics of innovation, adaptability, flexibility, emotional intelligence, technology, and systems thinking is clear—employers and employees must work together to close the gap in order to create a successful 21st century organization.

Why Organizations Are Not Having Their Needs Met

So many organizations today are in a state of stagnation without even realizing it. They have unmet needs that they don't even know exist—the need for adaptability and flexibility, increased diversity, and innovation. This condition of lacking creates a state of bewilderment. I have identified *what* the needs of the 21st century organization are in order to survive and thrive in a world of never ending change, but one question remains: *Why* are these needs going unmet?

The reason is a combination of factors, and no one branch of an organization is solely to blame. In part, it is due to organizations remaining *stuck in the past* with regard to how they operate, using 19th and 20th century business tactics in a 21st century world. However, this is generally because they have not been given the tools nor have they received the resources necessary to become a 21st century organization. It is also partially due to a tendency—a very human tendency that we all have at some time in our lives—to wish to remain in the status quo rather than embrace and integrate new approaches, both on the part of management and on the part of staff.

There is an old proverb that states, "Better the devil you know than the devil you don't." This applies to many people's feelings about change. Even if the status quo is not ideal, even when they can see that changes might be beneficial in some way, even when big positives may come from change, people fear the unknown. Many would rather maintain a state of complacency within the comfortable, familiar confines of the way things currently are than to take a risk and make a change. However, this tendency to huddle up and hide within the status quo and turn away from change can and does often hold people back, both on an individual level and collectively at the organizational level.

Willingness to embrace change is needed by both leadership and staff in order for an organization to find itself stepping beyond the status quo and into the realm of change. One way that staff can be encouraged to embrace change is by making them feel like, because they are, a valuable *part* of the changes in the organization. Embracing change as a constant doesn't mean culling the organizational herd, but rather, nurturing the organization's roots so that it can branch out and thrive in the modern era. When this happens, skills are addressed, and the gap closes a little.

Reluctance aside, there are practical reasons why companies want to hold on to their old ways of doing things. Let's explore those reasons.

One reason that established companies are reluctant to embrace change in procedure or practice is both the perceived and the real monetary cost involved in any change. The process of effecting a change involves planning, which involves time. Planning a company-wide change requires more than one person, and regardless of the passion for the company, unless you are the owner or *boss*, you expect to be paid for your time and, for the company, that translates to dollars. After the planning come the efforts to disseminate the ideas and plans for practicing these changes. This again takes additional time, which the short-sighted will see as loss of dollars. This, however, is not the case. While the initial facilitation and application of changes to forward-thinking approaches and practices may cost in man hours, the overall benefit is a more productive workforce, which ultimately increases the bottom line.

Further, reluctance to change is often because of the lack of acceptance of innovation by the founding members and the governing bodies of long-standing institutions or organizations. Some things should be held fast to, even in this forward-thinking and ever-changing world: Our values, core beliefs, and foundational principles help define us as individuals, families, communities, societies, governments, and businesses. However, a company built on the tradition of fair trade and industry can remain true to these beliefs and still change antiquated procedures and performances. A company whose mission statement includes "honesty, integrity, and customer service" would do well to incorporate current systems of innovative customer service that offer a wider variety of solutions to customer needs and satisfaction. Having a diverse group of thinkers and change makers on hand who believe in your company's mission statement will not only facilitate positive change, but also ensure your company's growth in the direction that you desire. This is a win for your company's clients, customers, and future.

Overall, the greatest and most prevalent reason for the resistance or reluctance to change is fear. Fear takes on many faces and oftentimes, the greater the change, the greater the fear. Leaders who follow outdated models of leadership and managerial styles often choose to stay where they are comfortable, and they can reasonably predict an outcome because fear says, "At least you know what the outcome will be if you stick with the status quo." Organizations that decide to forego changes in practice, personnel, or policy based on fear will find that their procrastination of the inevitable, because change is ultimately inevitable, will cost more in the long run in all areas of profit potential and employee morale.

Fear-based decisions are the least productive and the most likely to cause loss in every area of your organization, whether it is in your workforce potential or your bottom line. This is the dilemma of the skills gap, but thankfully, this gap can be bridged. In the next chapter, I will discuss how.

An Organization Defined and the Skills Gap

An *organization* is defined as "a body of people with a particular purpose," whether that purpose is business, education, government, civic, or pleasure. As I stated previously, there are six characteristics 21st century organizations will need to demonstrate competently in order to thrive in a 21st century world.

These characteristics are interwoven and interconnected, just like all the parts of an effective organization, and while they can be defined separately, their practical application includes part of all of them. Adaptability, technology, innovation, diversity, emotional intelligence, and systems thinking can bridge the skills gap in ways you might never anticipate, but as a leader, you must ask yourself the pivotal question: "Is it more important that we succeed my way, or that we accomplish success?"

Let's once again look at adaptability. Given the rates at which technological advances have occurred in the past century, the ability to adapt quickly to these inevitable changes and *roll with the punches* is of paramount importance for any organization. If the organization is to meet the demands of this century, they not only need to stay relevant in this present age, but especially if they want to thrive and prosper into the future. Affording your workforce the knowledge at your disposal is one way of effectively closing the skills gap. Sharing the information with your teams and expressing their importance in adapting to changes gives them a clearer picture of their importance, which further facilitates systems thinking as well.

The 21st century is the Knowledge Age. It is an era in which we have access to a world of knowledge in the most literal sense. The Internet has brought about globalization in a very real way, in both our personal lives and in the business world. Because of the Internet, telecommuting is possible and more common than ever.

This ability for us to connect with each other has given us all the unprecedented ability to keep in touch, moment-to-moment, no matter where we are. Keeping in contact with old friends who have moved abroad is easier than ever—and so is working for a company that is physically remote to you. So many jobs can now be performed via telecommuting that employees can be far more mobile than ever, which opens the door for a whole new workforce as well. Single moms or dads with the skill set for business, physically disabled persons who are homebound but equipped with technological or other abilities, and differently abled persons who may not fit in socially but are highly skilled and they meet your business' needs are now candidates for your company's labour force. Relocating employees to better suit your business needs or to meet their own personal needs is possible because their jobs follow them wherever they go. Additionally, telecommuting offers benefits to organizations, such as reduced stress in the workforce, a decline in absenteeism and tardiness, increased morale and productivity, and as identified above, it opens the doors for a more diverse workforce, and diversity is a fundamental characteristic of a 21st century organization.

Innovation is one characteristic that addresses the skills gap by creating an atmosphere of accessibility to information from anyplace that is *connected*. Rather than being limited to what is kept stored in libraries or encyclopedias, people are now able to open a web browser and query a search engine for information regarding any topic under the sun—and have thousands of results from thousands of sources across the globe returned in less than a second. This creates an incredible opportunity to which previous generations never had the privilege: the ability to connect with people *everywhere* and glean knowledge and learn skills from far-off corners of the world that were virtually unreachable. This globalization of our lifestyles on every level avails us to another one of the key things that enable an organization to keep up with modern-day demands: diversity. A diverse workforce is a ready workforce that includes a range of abilities, interests, and qualifications.

In the Industrial Revolution, it was quite fitting that workers were taught and adhered to strict standards of uniformity, as this was the safest and surest way to ensure the success of a mass produced item. Those days, however, are long gone.

As an organization and as a leader, you do not want employees who are all carbon copies of one another. Innovation demands a workforce that is diverse in gifts, passions, cultures, abilities, and talents. Diversity challenges the skills gap by bringing in a range of skills, and when allowed to flourish, your diverse workforce will meet more demands than you expected, in ways you never considered. Diversity means *variety*, and variety is simply a range of different things—quite the opposite of the standardization that is and has long been taught in traditional education models and expected in traditional workplace environments. Different skill sets can benefit an organization in unique ways, and one way to ensure that you have a variety of valuable skill sets within your organization is by hiring a variety of diverse *people*. By creating a diverse workplace, you are moving in the right direction to creating a successful workplace.

Diversity in the workplace is not a new concept, but what this word means has changed dramatically. In the 1950's, 60% of the

American workforce was white males. Men of other races made up the bulk of what was left, with a very small percentage being women. In the 1970's, diversity had come to mean around 40% women, with a small percentage of the whole being comprised of people of colour. Today's workplace diversity and that of the 21st century organization will come to mean corporations and businesses employ:

- Gender diversity
- Age diversity
- Racial diversity
- Differently abled diversity to include persons with psychological and physical disabilities
- Situational diversity to include family situations, such as single parents, those who care for disabled persons, or the elderly
- Sexual and political orientations diversity
- Ethnicity and cultural diversity

The 21st century workplace of diversity is not a utopian ideal that is impossible to reach. There will be bumps along the way as employees learn to work with others who look, think, and believe differently; however, this only mirrors what society is moving toward through globalization. Integrating the 21st century characteristics will lessen the depths of the bumps organizations may encounter.

While it is important to maintain a core value system and high standards, in order to be successful, people and organizations in the modern day must also be flexible rather than rigid in their acceptance of new ideas and technologies. Employing a person who works more efficiently at hours different than your operating hours is but one of many ways flexibility, innovation, technology, and diversity can close the skills gap. The staunchness and rigidity that typified the workplace of old has no place in the Knowledge

Age. Flexible scheduling, deference to forward thinking and teamwork, and adaptability to change are the traits of successful organizations, the leaders and managers, and all whom they employ. No longer are roles set in stone and standardized across the board. While titles and roles may still have some benefit, in a 21st century organization, roles transform according to the needs of the organization or business and according to the changes in the world at large, enabling people to become more than just their job descriptions. In the past, these titles may have seemed to lead to increase in productivity, but now lead only to stagnation. An adaptable, innovative, and diverse team doesn't need such antiquated labels in order to function at their highest level; they need only to know that their skills and ideas are important to the team and valued by their peers.

Communication, a key component in emotional intelligence, is another important skill set in today's workplace that can reduce the gap between what employees have and employers want. Rather than being rigid regarding how communication is conducted within an organization, business leaders must become adaptable with their communication styles and use the many forms of communication that modern technology has availed to them. Gone are the days of pen-to-paper and a telephone plugged into a wall being the main forms of communication within an organization. Even faxing—the 20th century *wave of the future*—is on the decline, now being replaced by email, text messaging, and instant messaging. Mobile phones, once a piece of technology utilized only by the elite, are now in practically every pocket in the developed world, and their capabilities go far beyond mere voice calling, allowing people to use various modes of communication while on the go—so that they can conduct business wherever they are at any given time. Cloud storage systems such as Skydrive, Box, Googledrive, and others allow the synchronization of data from anywhere across all devices and for all users. This technology, designed to facilitate the free exchange of ideas from all employees, is sorely underused simply because it is so new, and new can be so frightening. This is but one example of how newer forms of communication could influence productivity—*if only they were utilized*. Sharing information is one form of communication that is essential to an organization's success, but respectfully and effectively sharing ideas, responsibilities, and perspectives is an important part of a company's power and will be a buttress in bridging the skills gap.

Adaptability of leadership, management, and staff, a diverse workforce with equally diverse skills and bases of knowledge, flexibility, and an open view toward forms and styles of communication, all these things combine to create what might be the most important attributes that an organization needs to bridge the assumed skills gap and thrive in the 21st century: innovation and systems thinking. Having a diverse and adaptable team that has the ability to communicate, however and whenever they need to in order to get their jobs done, reflects an organization that facilitates innovation—and innovation is a necessary part of being a successful organization in today's ever-changing world. To stay significant in this world of constant change, an organization needs to facilitate change in their leadership and in their workforce. Not just once, but repeatedly—constantly. That is the nature of the Knowledge Age: constant change, perpetual newness. Embracing new things and new ideas—and encouraging them to keep on coming—is the key to maintaining relevance in a world that is continuously in a state of flux.

There is indeed a skills gap in organizations today, but that can be bridged. There is no right or wrong side of this; there are only two parts to a whole. When organizations and their workforce finally accept this, then there will be a hopeful beginning. The skills gap dilemma has been discussed in Chapter 3, and in Chapter 4, I will further discuss the tools for bridging the skills gap.

"Change can be beautiful when we are brave enough to evolve with it, and change can be brutal when we fearfully resist it." ~ *Bryant McGill*

Chapter 4: Tools for Bridging the Skills Gap

"The illiterate of the 21st century will not be those who cannot read and write, but those who cannot learn, unlearn, and relearn." ~ Alvin Toffler

So far on this journey, I have provided some perspective on the past and the foundations of modern business and organizational practices. I introduced you to six important characteristics that must be present in a 21st century organization in order for it to flourish in this constantly changing global economy, and I have discussed how the old and the new approaches have created a perceived skills gap. Now, let's take a look at how to bridge the gap and create an organization that is on a solid plane for now and the future.

As I mentioned in Chapter 3, a skills gap exists in many organizations. The divide between the skills necessary to keep up with modern innovation and the skills being produced through our educational system is a wide chasm.

It is not, however, one that cannot be bridged with new approaches in business philosophy, training, and practical application. Some ways to bridge the gap include, but are not limited to:

- Transforming academic curriculum to include 21st century approaches and important studies, such as:
    - critical thinking
    - emotional intelligence and communication skills
    - decision making and analytical skills
    - personal accountability
    - multiple intelligence

- coding
- Summer internship programs for high school juniors and seniors as well as college students
- Use of new forms of online education, such as a nanodegree
- Mentorship programs
- Professional development and skills guidance for employees
- Leadership seminars
- Revamp hiring practices, job descriptions, and employee expectations

While this list is not exhaustive, it does offer some ideas for progress. Let's discuss them in a little more detail.

Education in the 21st Century

Primary education is paramount in bridging the skills gap for our future employees and business leaders. This is a foundational change that will be far reaching. Organizations with the insight and fortitude to invest in these changes will reap the rewards in many ways, such as increased community support, brand and name recognition in association with good works, and good old fashioned *karma*.

The goal of primary education has long been *job readiness*, but as the four C's (culture for learning, critical thinking skills, communication skills, and coding skills) meet the three R's, (reading, writing, and arithmetic), we have to re-evaluate the process by which all people are taught. Because most public school systems were created to meet the needs of the many in the most standardized way, as a result, a skills gap exists here as well. As in any organization, considering a person's strengths and weaknesses is crucial to helping them excel. When public education in all communities begins to embrace the changes necessary to become a 21st century organization itself, then we will truly be on the way to closing the skills gap and becoming a global society.

Internships, both paid and unpaid, provide skills training, work experience, and opportunities for mentorship. High school juniors and seniors are prime candidates for internships. Forward-thinking companies will create opportunities for these young minds to get a glimpse of what possibilities lay beyond graduation and offer scholarships and further training to those promising candidates who successfully complete their internship. By providing internships the organization is essentially preparing the people they want to walk through their doors. When that individual is offered a taste of your culture and innovation they will be your new pioneers who are eager to come back and share their ideas with your organization.

While an internship programs is helping young people to obtain practical knowledge, both leaders and employees in participating organizations will have the opportunity to practice their leadership skills in this internship scenario. They will be given the opportunity to train others, to encourage and support someone who cannot repay them in kind, and to find compassion for those who think differently than themselves among other things. This win-win scenario lays the foundation for skilled employees later, while helping young people to envision their successful future in a 21st century economy.

Another type of internship program is a *college co-op program*. Some of these programs allow the student to attend classes one semester and work the next, while some allow for the student to work part time and attend class part time. Generally, at the end of the internship program, the student works at the host company for an agreed-upon amount of time, which again creates a scenario where both parties benefit from the arrangement.

Professional development is an effective tool in bridging the skills gap. In-house education is one way to help employees and leaders in your company to improve their skills or acquire new ones. Having in-house education makes sense for large organizations that want to bring their workforce up to current standards and create confident and capable employees and leaders from all levels. One benefit of in-house continuing education is that your employees are learning specific to your needs and on your time table.

Other sources of continuing education that can effectively bridge the gap are community college courses, local universities, seminars and conferences, and both traditional online education and a new form of industry-specific online degree plans called nanodegrees. This vocational degree plan is offering a far more affordable way for underfunded students or displaced workers to gain the skills necessary to enter today's job market with confidence and ability.

Another very practical way for organizations to close the skills gap is to assess and amend their own hiring practices. Twenty-first century organizations have need of specific skills and their hiring practices—the way they advertise for new employees to their lists of job descriptions must reflect these current needs. Recruitment of skills-specific groups rather than degree-specific groups will net a greater return on investment as well as facilitate promoting from within your organization. An employee who has excelled in customer service and teambuilding and has an interest in an open position is a great candidate for skills-specific training and will very likely be more loyal and proactive than a new recruit.

The interview process is an effective place to determine if a candidate is right for your 21st century company. The interview process is where you find that just because Mr. Smith looks smashing in his new suit and graduated in the top 10% of his class in business school, he may not necessarily be the right fit for your organization. A personnel manager who knows her/his company's work culture, the specifics of the posted job, and the team with which the candidate will be working is one who can most effectively ascertain if an applicant is the perfect fit for the job.

Another innovative option when recruiting is working with an employment services agency where their focus is to do *job matching,* they work directly with employer providing the employer with several candidates to choose from who "match" the culture and skills that the employer is seeking. In some cases the *match* may not be someone the employer would have considered due to a previous work injury, a disability or even a past criminal record. However, the *match* offers a trial period for the employer to observe the individual without commitment; this opportunity is not only a benefit for the employer to discern if the individual fits within the organizational culture it also allows a person to have a second chance to prove to themselves and others that they are employable.

Globalization is a Must

Another skills gap that exists is that of global awareness. The term globalization as it pertains to business refers to the increasing integration and relationship of companies, employees, and customers or clients in countries all over the world, rather than domestic only. With the walls crashing down around business every day, globalization is essential to success, but what does global awareness or a global approach to business look like?

A global approach to business includes:

- Diversity
- Inclusiveness
- Cultural awareness
- Technologically adept employees

How does a 21st century organization benefit from *inclusiveness*, and how does this impact the skills gap problem? Inclusiveness helps in every facet of business by utilizing the gifts, talents, and skills of each employee at every level. This radical consideration of each person and what he or she brings to the table impassions people to "bring their A game." Consider for a moment how you react or respond when you know you are accepted versus when you are unsure going into a situation, whether business or personal. If you are like most people, you feel and act confident when you know that your ideas and contributions will be welcomed, while you feel or behave pensively and with caution when you are uncertain. This is a natural phenomenon in every life form: proceeding with prudence when uncertainty lurks. In business, however, hesitation because of fear, indecision, or ambiguity can be quite costly. This is not in any way suggesting that businesses should throw caution to the wind and act recklessly; on the contrary, instead, this thinking advocates counsel and support from all parts of your organization.

Diversity is another global approach to business whose time has come. As discussed in the previous chapter, diversity no longer refers only to race, gender, and cultural differences. Now the term includes a broader definition that includes thoughts, abilities, and personalities, among other things. Diversity in the workplace in the 21st century includes embracing differences and encouraging problem solving through natural tendencies. For example, some people are really well spoken; they enjoy an audience and can hold a client's attention for hours on end with their silver tongue and rapier wit. Others, however, prefer a monitor and a keyboard with endless lines of code. One is no more or less important to an organization's success, and often, the success of each relies on the cooperation of each with the whole.

Gender, age, racial, ethnic, and sexual diversity are not only good business practice now, but in most instances, they are also law in the United States and Canada. The U.S. Equal Employment Opportunity Commission (as cited in FindLaw, 2014) has stated,

> Title VII of the Civil Rights Act of 1964, prohibits an employer with fifteen or more employees from discriminating on the basis of race, national origin, gender, or religion. Under Title VII, it is illegal for an employer to take any of the following actions against an employee based upon his or her race, national origin, gender, or religion. (para. 2)

Further, the Americans with Disabilities Act and the Rehabilitation Act prohibit discrimination based on a person's disabilities and the Immigration Reform and Control Act forbid discrimination based on an employees or prospective employees' national origin. An Executive Order, 13087, signed by President Bill Clinton in 1998 amended the Equal Employment Opportunity Act and was further amended by Executive Order by President Barak Obama in July 2014 that prohibited discrimination based on sexual orientation and gender identity.

While the laws governing equal opportunity employment may not be the same in all lands and cultures, globalization will require that each company ascribe to these principals or face the frustration of being left behind in the business arena at the very least.

Sensitivity to cultural norms will be weighty when doing business on a global level, and this will come more naturally in an environment of diversity and inclusion. The diverse 21st century workplace is not a utopian ideal that is impossible to reach. There will be hiccups along the way as employees adjust the way they work with others who look, think, and believe differently; however, this only mirrors what society is moving toward through globalization and will eventually benefit every part of your organization and the societies in which you do business.

As I stated earlier, cultural awareness is a part of diversity and inclusiveness. How exactly does this help your business though?

In a global organization, your awareness of your customers is vital. Knowing firsthand what products, images, and ad campaigns will work in each culture can be the difference between a winning business move and a catastrophe. If you don't have a foreknowledge of the cultures in which your clients live, you may offend your customer or discredit your company. Hurt feelings can foster resentment for a very long time in business and governments, and the Internet has extremely long memories.

These are just a few of the tools that may be useful in bringing your organization into the 21st century business model. While incorporating any one will change the dynamics of your company, including as many as possible will be more beneficial. Your workforce will show more job readiness and strength of character as they learn that they are an integral part of your business. As you learn more about your employees and their abilities, you may also learn that the gap is not nearly as wide as you thought.

Now, let's take a look at innovation and how it plays a role in your business' future.

Chapter 5: The 21st Century Approach to Innovation

"Collaboration is important not just because it's a better way to learn. The spirit of collaboration is penetrating every institution and all of our lives. So learning to collaborate is part of equipping yourself for effectiveness, problem solving, innovation, and life-long learning in an every changing networked economy." ~ Don Tapscott

As we continue our journey toward the development of a dynamic and fruitful 21st century organization, I would be remiss if I neglected to emphasize the importance of innovation and how vitally necessary it is to your company's future. To be innovative, simply, is to use new ideas or methods, but innovation is not always a perceived as a *simple* thing.

Innovation Wasn't Always Welcomed

It is small wonder why the world is so ready for a change to innovative thinking in the workplace. In the 19th and 20th centuries, workers who stepped out of place were punished physically, including hitting, slapping, shoving, beatings, loss of breaks (which was a substantial loss since breaks were rare and were the only time eating, resting, or toilet needs were addressed), or even in the case of women, cutting off their hair.

Later, when we became *civilized*, verbal assaults, character assassinations, and public criticism were the acceptable forms of punishment for failing to meet quotas, failure to perform, or failure to follow instructions. These practices produced a society of persons who were full of resentment and even anger. Often, since they had to *take it* at work in order to continue working and in most cases to earn the money to survive, they took that resentment into their communities and homes. Anger and resentment tend to be contagious, even if those infected don't understand how or why they have become a part of the process.

The mentality created by such practices produced not only resentful workers, but also workers who stayed for a paycheque, not a purpose. A workforce that cares only for their pay is one who will do the least amount of work possible and complete work that has been specifically assigned to them, leaving tasks undone and profits unrealized. This workforce, while able to function at much higher levels, externally they appear lazy and unmotivated, even unintelligent, though they hold answers to questions, problems, and ideas for a better way right there inside of them.

The 21st century approach to innovation will require leaders to experience not only a change of mind, but also a change of heart.

Passion is a big part of innovation. It is the mindset that says, "We all matter" and "No one is unimportant in our organization," and then backs those statements up with action. Innovation not only embraces change, but also encourages it and fosters a sense of welcome for change agents to think, grow, and do the impossible. Innovation communicates effectively and efficiently, producing an openness and consideration, where understanding can turn into ideas and ideas can turn into marketable products and services. Innovation allows for mistakes, failures, and further attempts at greatness because innovation doesn't allow setbacks to be stopping places, only resting places for comebacks to be created.

Mistakes are the wave of the future. Yes, you read that correctly. Mistakes are important, and until organizations and businesses release the fear of making a mistake and allow freedom in thought and creativity, they will remain stagnate. So many of our current comforts were created only after repeated failed attempts:

- Thomas Edison was considered by his teachers as "too stupid to learn anything" and is famous for failing 1,000 times to invent the light bulb. He did, however, eventually invent the light bulb and held 1,093 patents in the United States, as well as patents in France, Germany, and the United Kingdom. This prolific inventor did not give up, and we are all very grateful for that when night falls.
- American President Abraham Lincoln failed as a businessman, he failed at being an attorney, and he even failed in his first attempts at politics, but he did not give up, and he became one of the most important presidents in American history.
- Henry Ford failed to the point of bankruptcy, five times, but succeeded in becoming a pioneer in mass production and eventually became a great American success story.
- R.H. Macy of the Macy Department Store success failed seven times before his idea became a success, and Macy's Department Store in New York grew from a dry goods store to one that created made-to-order clothing in their onsite factory.
- Fred Smith, the founder of Federal Express, received a grade of C on his college paper describing his idea for his overnight delivery service. The professor explained that his idea wasn't feasible. Today, that same idea that was graded so poorly resulted in $45.57 BILLION in sales/revenue in the 2014 fiscal year.

There are so many more examples of *failed* successes that one book couldn't contain it, but the point remains that when people are allowed to think and create new ideas, they will encounter failure. The ones who succeed are the ones who keep thinking, trying, and have people around them to encourage them and help them to realize their dreams. When your organization becomes a place where people can think freely and fail then try again, amazing things can happen.

The Organization of the 21st Century Must Foster Innovation

In the past, each member of a company had a specific function and was encouraged to do that function and that function alone. If you were a file clerk and you saw a need for the coffee urn to be refilled, you went to the personnel assigned to make coffee to let them handle that task. A janitor who saw a loose screw was not encouraged to take out his screw driver and fix it on the spot, but instead to create a work order and send it to the appropriate office. Days or even weeks later that screw might get fixed by a maintenance person. Because of the chain of command, all of the ideas, concerns, or complaints that are introduced must go through meetings and committees and weeks of discussion before they ever see a response. In that amount of time, dreams can die of neglect. Ideas run out of air and suffocate. Possibilities tend to float away and end up in other lands more ready to grasp the potential and turn it into reality.

The idea of 21st century innovation is that within reason, if we see a problem and have a solution, we work to fix it and not leave it where it stands; the employee's innovative idea is not limited by saying, "That's not in my job description." The resulting efficiency did not have to wait for numerous levels of meeting to be implemented. Rather than climbing up a bureaucratic ladder with the proposed solution, forced to obtain clearance from multiple managers in order to follow through with the fix, the employee is free to implement his or her solution as soon as it is conceived, thus saving copious amounts of time. In reducing wasted time alone, 21st century organizations will recoup financial losses. Not surprisingly, job descriptions will naturally need to be revamped for the 21st century organization.

Formerly, job descriptions were the boxes that kept creativity stifled. They were created by a well-meaning innovator of his time, Fredrick Taylor, who sought to improve industrial efficiency and did this so well that his practices became a system called *scientific management* that is still used today in many places and practices. The reason that job descriptions have become outdated, however, is that technology moves with such breakneck speed today that by the time a job description has been formalized, the parameters have changed. Additionally, a job description cannot contain every piece of an innovative thinker's job. Jobs in the 21st century organization are constantly reshaping and often multi-dimensional. In revamping this useful tool, it will become a more broadly formed document that will help to navigate an employee, but not dictate a position in a company.

Another 21st century approach that will be innovative is that of communication. Where once there seemed to be a *management says and everyone jumps* mentality, now there must be a more effective form of communication.

Communication skills are learned and perfected by practice like most other skills, but this practice must take place in a culture of acceptance. Verbal and non-verbal communication skills are incredibly important in life, and for the purposes of a 21st century organization, they are even more important. Poor communication often leads to dissention in the form of misunderstandings, hurt feelings, power struggles, and indecision. Workplace dissention slows down productivity and sorely limits creativity. Proficient communication skills, however, lead to valuable relationships between team members, leaders, and customers. When someone believes that they are being heard and understood, they become passionate about sharing.

As passion increases, and it will as innovative thinking is fostered, a sense of purpose will grow as well. Imagine an engaged workplace where your workforce is excited about coming to work, enjoys the time they spend at the office, and smiles while they are there. It happens even now in companies like Google, who has been named the top company to work for many times over the years. They are an innovative company whose culture is one of innovation, flexibility, and responsiveness. Their employees want to come to work; they want to not only stay employed there, but they also look forward to growing in the company. SAS, another software company, comes in next at number two for many of the same reasons. But suppose your organization doesn't create software, perhaps yours is a widget factory or a trash collection business. It doesn't matter what service you provide or product you create; if you do it with passion and innovation, you will do it well. People, both customers and employees, and everyone else, respond to greatness, and greatness grows in a place where creativity, communication, and innovation are welcome.

While the greatest innovation will be in the people you employ, you can influence these people quite effectively by offering an environment that will spark or facilitate originality, creativity, and inspiration.

According to Dr. Stuart Brown, founder of the National Institute for Play, "There is good evidence that if you allow employees to engage in something they want to do, (which) is playful, there are better outcomes in terms of productivity and motivation" (as cited in Tarkin, 2012, para. 3).

Every workplace, new and old, consists of people, processes, and practices, and whether your organization is one that builds, buys, or brings change, all businesses have a product. Yours might be intellectual property, wealth, or rocket ships, but all organizations have produced something. No matter the product, the people are the most important asset. Innovative processes and practices will help the people to create the product more effectively. So let's look at some innovative practices that can help your greatest asset, which is your people, in the process of producing what all businesses want: success.

Create a workplace that is innovative by cultivating an environment of problem solving

Most people are natural problem solvers when there is a reward on the other side of their problem. Infants have problem solving skills:

> *Problem*: "I'm wet and hungry, and I don't like it."
>
> *Reward for solving problem*: Food in my tummy and dry clothes.
>
> *Solution*: Scream until someone identifies my problem and fixes it.

Not a very effective solution for an adult, but the example supports the claim that most people are innate problem solvers.

Somewhere along the way though, we are trained out of this natural ability. Whether it was because we were trained by those who needed to feel secure in their position or wanted to be the hero who rode in to save the day and solved the problems, 21st century organizations don't have time for that sort of mentality. We all have to be problems solvers, and that skill can be reanimated in most of your employees by creating a place where problem solving is rewarded—but people can't solve a problem they don't know exists. Unlike *Titanic thinking*, where the leaders keep the problems a secret in order to avoid an onslaught panic, 21st century business leaders will make the problems available to their greatest resource for solving them: their workforce.

One possibility might be a *problems/ideas board*, where any problem or situation that needs a resolution can be added for all to see. Maybe your organization would be more responsive to an email, or text, or even a digital display. However the word gets out, if everyone knows there is a problem to be solved, they can all be a part of the solution.

In the past, rewards have been simply monetary remuneration in the form of bonuses, vacation time, or benefits, but an innovative office will create rewards that are fun as well. Perhaps your teams will have a weekly contest to see who has the most creative ideas regarding a company-wide problem. Maybe you buy lunch or dinner for the winning team, or even better, let the winner choose from a surprise bag of gift cards to local eateries. That way everyone is surprised, there is an element of fun, and they can choose to use the card, give it away, or donate it to charity. An element of fun and reward is a great process for promoting the practice of problem solving among your people.

Archaeology professor and author Brian D. Hayden has discussed the significance of celebratory meals in his book, *The Power of Feasts* (2014). He suggests that the practice of feasting is more than just a fancy dinner party—it is a display of success. Traditionally, political entities and individuals in power would hold feasts in order to show that they had a surplus that they could share with the larger community. This demonstration of surplus was a way in which those people in power could show others that they were successful enough to share their wealth with others. This same concept can be applied to leaders within an organization who show their appreciation of staff members who have gone above and beyond by taking their department out for a celebratory luncheon. By celebrating successes with a feast, leaders show that they are sharing in the successes of their staff, thus sharing solidarity with their team members. These celebrations encourage high performance from staff members by showing that such performance will be rewarded—and according to Hayden's deductions, the reward itself is a display of the success of the team.

Create a happy place

Another great practical way to encourage a sense of innovation in the workplace is to create a *happy place*. A happy place is a stress-free zone where employees will take a *happy break*. This place might be a room where employees can play a game or a guitar, write a letter or make a phone call, or be alone or with others. It might be a quiet place like the nap pods at all of Google's facilities, an indoor skate bowl like Comvert in Milan, Italy, or a 5-story atrium that houses a 3-story slide like Corus Quay in Toronto, Canada. Some other innovative ideas to create a stress-free environment or an environment where stress can be diffused might be an onsite garden, perhaps a rooftop sanctuary where pets are welcome. Maybe a billiards table, a walking path through the grounds, or a swing in the break room is your cup of tea. Your workforce might prefer a gym, a library, or a place where the music is so loud the problems can't get through the sound barrier, but whatever spells happy to your employees, it is in your organization's best interest. Whatever the space looks like to your organization, the outcome must be to help your employees to distress and get *happy* because a happy workforce is far more productive and creative and able to meet their goals for your organization.

Encourage a healthy lifestyle

Encouraging your workforce to remain or become healthy is a practical way to bring a sense of innovation to your workplace and workforce. The focus has been, for at least the past decade or so, on getting healthier. Many workplaces have already begun to add gym memberships or reimbursements for such to employees who are willing to embrace healthy lifestyle changes. Creating an onsite cafeteria is a great way to help your staff to eat healthier or encourage better diets through discounts to local eateries that offer healthier choices. Smaller facilities can provide healthy snacks or, at the very least, change the standard junk food fare in the vending machines to that with lower fat and salt. However, physical health is only one part of a person's health. Mental health is of vital importance in all aspects of a person's life, including the workplace. According to the Canadian Centre for Occupational Health and Safety (2012), psychological support tops their list of the 13 organizational factors that impact organizational health (para. 4).

It is important that workers feel supported psychologically in order to adopt the systems mentality that is needed in a 21st century organization. When we feel supported, we are more readily available and willing to support others and our host entity, the organization. Some practical ways to provide mental and psychological support in the work place are to offer onsite counseling and Employee Assistance Programs, *well-being days* (also known as "mental health days"), or in-house seminars on common stressors and how to cope with them. As the 21st century characteristic of inclusiveness is embraced and peoples of all cultures are encountered in our more global community, we will find that the masks we all hid behind previously are more readily shed. If you serve people, work with or for people, or employ people, then you will encounter mental or psychological health issues. As with our problem-solving skills, our psychosocial skills can be sharpened and must be for a healthier 21st century existence.

An important innovative practice that will help employees in their method to happy and healthy is *flexible scheduling*. This innovative practice allows for earlier or later hours of business, a focus on the ends rather than the means, and allows an employee to work, within reason, when and where they feel best and are able to produce the best results. This may be in the cafeteria or that new innovative garden space you created. It may be on the treadmill or the subway because the 21st century organization realizes that technology and innovation are partners in a productive workforce, and that productivity is a 24-hour-a-day possibility.

As I conclude this chapter on innovation, it is important to note that innovation by its own definition will require constant consideration of new ideas, ways, and practices. This will become easier as time goes on because your organization will become one that not only accepts but also *creates* innovative new ideas and techniques and practices of their own.

In the next chapter, I will look at leadership in the 21st century and how embracing the key characteristics of a 21st century organization will help you to become a more effective and productive leader.

"Learning and innovation go hand in hand. The arrogance of success is to think that what you did yesterday will be sufficient for tomorrow." ~ *Williams Pollard*

Chapter 6: Leadership in the 21st Century

"The past is to be respected and acknowledged, but not worshipped; it is our future in which we will find our greatness."
~ Pierre Trudeau

It has been established that organizations must be open to change, growth, and adaptation in order to maintain their viability in the modern age. Leadership within those organizations must also undergo changes in order to stay afloat. It is not enough to enact changes and stand by, watching the transitions as they unfold. Change must come from all levels, and it begins at the top. In this chapter, I will take a look at traditional leadership models, discuss their benefits and drawbacks, and contrast them with models of leadership that are better-suited to an organization that wishes to stay afloat in the 21st century.

Traditional Leadership

In the past, the concept of *leadership* was very straightforward: One person or one elite group of select people led, and others followed. Leaders gave orders, and others carried out those orders. Leaders dictated how business was to be conducted, and others took on the task of making it so. Leaders were at the top of the hierarchy, and all others were on levels below them. Leaders had the power and control, they had sway—and everyone else was to do as leaders bade them to do.

This leadership model has been a commonplace one throughout the history of industry, and it prevails even now for many organizations. However, this *top-down* form of leadership, although useful at one point in time (for the purposes of standardization and safety measures, as well as the ability to pinpoint accountability and responsibility), has become archaic in this day and age. The 21st century corporation is not a coal mine. No longer are staff members content to be cogs turning within a machine, silently doing their part to keep the organization functional—nor should they be. After all, they may have something of greater value to offer, but—finding themselves lacking an outlet for their great ideas or valuable skills—they become embittered, feeling as though their merits are going unused and undetected as they carry out their job duties like machines. This creates an unfortunate scenario for people at all levels within the organization. The leaders miss out on the opportunity to utilize the full range of skills that their staff have, skills which could be put to good use and be beneficial to the growth of the organization. The staff members come to feel undervalued and disgruntled, which in turn has a negative impact on work productivity. It is a lose/lose situation—for leaders, for staff, and for the organization as a whole.

It is natural for people to resist change (and all that comes along with it). We become accustomed to the status quo: It is a familiar place and one that we know like the backs of our hands. However, the tendency to stay within the comfort zone of the status quo, embracing the *known* and feeling hesitant to even contemplate the *unknown* can lead to inertia. There is no room for stagnation in the whirlwind of change that is the 21st century.

Leaders whose organizations are maintaining their success by continuing to do what they have always done may find themselves thinking, "Why fix what isn't broken? What we are doing now is working for our organization and has been working for us for years. Why wouldn't it continue to work for years to come?" I counter these questions with a question of my own: Why wait until something is broken and needs to be fixed, rather than taking a proactive approach and staying one step ahead? Many organizations are in a reactive mode, and as a result they have an exhausted workforce lashing out or passively resisting change.

Those who wait for a *fall* find themselves clambering to get back up to the top, and they may find that by that time, it is too late to reclaim what has been lost in the fall. Those with the foresight to see what will is necessary in order to maintain relevance in the Knowledge Age, however, need not suffer a fall, nor will they need to scramble to regain their proverbial footing when change is finally inevitable. Rather, they can *keep* their organizations relevant by taking note of what leads to success for 21st century organizations and enacting changes accordingly.

Leadership in a 21st Century Organization

There are many models for leadership, but not all of them are suitable for an organization that wants to be on the forefront in the 21st century. There is a need to pull away from traditional leadership models, for even though they served their purpose in the past, those days are gone, and the new era calls for reform, starting with approaches to leadership. Let's discuss some of the leadership models that we see businesses utilizing today, and explore some of the benefits and drawbacks to each style: transactional leadership, transformational leadership, bureaucratic leadership vs. charismatic leadership, and vertical leadership vs. horizontal leadership.

Transactional leadership: A thing of the past?

Transactional leadership, also called *managerial leadership*, is a leadership style that is most concerned with making transactions within a business efficient and productive. This style of leadership is one that concerns itself with keeping the proverbial rigging taut and is well-suited to maintaining the status quo. This was a very useful style of leadership for prior generations and continues to be a valuable form of leadership for certain types of organizations. For example, the floor manager of a large chain retailer who oversees dozens of employees will be deeply concerned with keeping a running tally of the day's earnings, keeping tabs on which employees are doing what and when, and offering rewards to employees who adhere diligently to the rulebook while offering consequences to employees whose behaviour has a negative impact on the continued smooth-running operation of the store (such as writing up an employee who is habitually late coming back from his or her lunch break). When goals are clearly defined in strict, regimented terms and little innovation is needed, transactional leaders are the people to get the job done right. A transactional leadership style is useful for keeping well-functioning, small-scale operations well-oiled—it is the leadership style for maintaining rather than innovating. If the supervisor for the aforementioned hypothetical retail store has no interest in creating a new and exciting way of ringing up purchases, the transactional leadership style will be perfectly sufficient for his or her business needs. When it is of more value for a process to remain the same than it is for a process to be continuously renewed and refreshed, the rigidity of the transactional leadership style proves to be quite useful. The motto of the transactional leadership style could be something akin to "Keep up the good work—but don't rock the boat."

Transformational leadership: The wave of the future

Whereas transactional leadership is localized and strictly regimented, transformational leadership is just what the name implies: It is focused on transforming business operations in order to revamp and refresh. Transformational leaders are concerned with renewal and innovation, finding the newest and best way to perform a process. A transformational leadership style is very well-suited to the 21st century organization, as it is in alignment with the 21st century values of adaptability, flexibility, innovation, and diversity. Transformational leaders are people with a vision—a vision involving change. Thus, it is the perfect leadership style for a modern-day organization's executive cabinet to adopt. The motto of the transformational leadership style could be something along the lines of "Inspiration and vision are the keys to growth, forward momentum and positive change."

Bureaucratic leadership vs. charismatic leadership

The bureaucratic leadership style is one that is deeply concerned with rules and regulations and strict adherence to those rules and regulations. This form of leadership is quite limiting, both to the leaders themselves and their employees, in that it leaves little room for growth, change, and diversity. However, bureaucratic leadership does have its place: Organizations that deal in extremely hazardous work, such as mining or work involving hazardous materials are well-served by having strictly regulated rules in place for the purposes of safety. Yet, many organizations utilize this leadership style even though it is to their detriment. Not all organizations can benefit from rigid bureaucracy, particularly in an era where growth and flexibility are becoming the new norm.

Charismatic leadership, on the other hand, is a style of leadership that leaves employees feeling inspired and motivated due to the charismatic example set by their leader. A charismatic leader can sway his or her staff members in the direction of his or her vision for the organization, purely with the force of his or her presence. Rather than wielding an iron fist of power, the charismatic leader draws the team in with an appealing image or ideal. This form of leadership is commonly used by politicians, as creating an image and beckoning to potential followers with a charming demeanor is very useful in the political game. However, charismatic leadership can have its drawbacks. If the leader's vision is self-serving, for example, it may not be a vision that encourages organizational innovation, thus creating a potentially detrimental situation for the organization itself.

Horizontal leadership vs, vertical leadership

If the status quo of the top-down leadership model is not going to be beneficial for a 21st century organization, what will be? Where does the solution to the dilemma lie? I propose that rather than using the traditional, hierarchical, vertical forms of leadership, organizations adopt a horizontal or lateral model of leadership, wherein decision-making comes from all sides.

This horizontal leadership model improves upon the vertical leadership model in several ways. Let's take a deeper look.

Horizontal leadership saves time

When an organization re-works its leadership system from a hierarchical approach to a horizontal approach, it can save time for everyone in the company. By enabling staff members to have a say in decision-making processes pertaining to the performance of their jobs, there is a cutting out of the middleman. No longer do employees have to wait for the go-ahead from their managers for every little change that they may wish to implement—rather, they are permitted to use their best judgment in order to make a decision that will be beneficial to all. This eliminates the need to play the waiting game while the higher-ups place their stamp of approval on a proposed course of action and send it back down the ranks.

Horizontal leadership boosts morale

To quote French philosopher Jean-Paul Sartre, "Only the guy who isn't rowing has time to rock the boat." In other words, people who are busy putting their skills to work don't have the time nor inclination to make metaphorical waves. When staff members are given more freedom to use their judgment in the performance of their job duties, they come to feel that their input is truly valuable. When people feel like they have a say in how their jobs get done and when they feel like their feedback is being listened to and implemented, they feel less like easily replaced spokes in a wheel and more like esteemed members of a team. This is incredibly good for the overall level of morale within an organization, as people want to feel like they matter—and those who feel like they matter are less likely to be lackluster in their performance at work than those who feel overlooked, uncared about, and not valuable to their organization or its leaders. When employees feel that they have a space within which they can have their voices be heard, they feel like they matter and that their feedback can and will leave an imprint upon the organization that employs them.

Horizontal leadership facilitates innovation

The horizontal leadership model allows more people to have a hand in the direction the organization is moving in. In this way, innovation is facilitated. By having a more diverse group of people offering their input and putting their unique skill sets actively to work, new ideas can spring forth and be implemented with the greatest of ease. The more people you have giving voice to their ideas, the more likelihood there is of a bright, new idea coming to light—an idea that may set your organization ahead of the curve.

The concept of servant leadership

If traditional forms of leadership are seen as a sort of power play in which a select few people have most of the control within an organization and use employees to serve their own needs, servant leadership is a complete 180-degree turnaround from that leadership model. Rather than demanding the service of *underlings* to comply with their desires, servant leaders seek to give service to their employees. In this way, servant leadership is almost a total reversal of the traditional, vertical leadership model. Servant leadership involves giving back to the organization and helping individuals within it who may be at a disadvantage. Servant leadership has its roots deep within morality: The servant leader wants to enact positive changes by aiding those in his or her employ, with the belief that the acts of service will themselves inspire and motivate others to do likewise. This form of leadership is well-suited to leaders of organizations that have a basis in religion or that work with disadvantaged members of the public, such as indigent populations.

Parallels between leadership types and styles

The hierarchical leadership model, wherein the *top dog* wields the majority of power within an organization and essentially dictates the way business shall be conducted within that organization, has parallels with the transactional leadership approach. Both involve control being firmly in the hand of a *higher-up*, with power trickling down through the ranks from above. Both involve a highly regulated, systematic approach to leadership, and both are concerned with delegation of power and tasks, leaving little room for outside input from those who are lowest on the metaphorical totem pole. The bureaucratic leadership style also lends itself well to a hierarchical leadership setup and tends to be seen often where transactional leadership is present. Charismatic leaders can be seen in all leadership models—from bureaucratic and autocratic to democratic and from transactional to transformational.

The lateral leadership model, wherein an organization's totem pole of power gets toppled and turned on its side, allowing for input on decision-making from all staff members in all roles, is very much in synchrony with the transformational leadership style. Both facilitate change and innovation by *shaking things up*, doing away with the traditional ways of approaching business decisions, and opening a listening ear to people who would otherwise not be heard. Both embrace the potential for positive opportunities by doing away with the *old way* of keeping a tight rein on underlings and keeping control firmly in hand. Both welcome the chance to foster the growth of employees at all levels of the organization, recognizing that said individual growth could well lead to the growth of the organization as a whole.

Characteristics of an Effective 21st Century Leader

What qualities are needed in order to effectively lead an organization in today's world? There are a few key characteristics that a modern leader should possess in order to lead competently in the Knowledge Age are presented in this discussion: lead by example, be open-minded, communicate well, embrace technology, and be willing to sacrifice for the greater good.

Lead by example

American businessman and philanthropist Ray Kroc once said that "the quality of a leader is reflected in the standards they set for themselves." Although he passed away long before the 20th century was over, Kroc was ahead of his time, as he knew that in order to be effective as a leader, one must lead by example. It is not enough to tell people what to do; one must show them what to do—and whatever standards you hold your staff to, you must first and foremost hold yourself to. Whatever qualities you would like to see in your employees should first be qualities that you possess, so that you can exemplify that which you desire from other members of your organization's team.

Be open-minded

Keeping an open mind is crucial for the success of a leader in this day and age. Rigidity and closed-mindedness only lead to stagnation. Being open to new ideas creates opportunities for tangible improvement and innovation. Trading in the *my way or the highway* approach to leadership for an approach that is receptive to outside views helps to ensure that you are doing all you can to move the organization forward. Sometimes, the best way to hold onto your leadership role is by letting go of some of the control that you wield within that role and allowing others to share their perspectives on how to proceed with a given situation.

Communicate well

I cannot stress the importance of communication enough. Leaders need to make sure that they are being heard and understood, and since communication is a two-way street, they must also make sure that they are hearing and understanding what is being said to them. In the *old days*, communication methods were very limited; if you wanted to get in touch with someone about a pressing business matter 50 years ago, phone or fax were your only two options. Today, we have myriad options for communication methods, such as email, instant messaging, Skype, text messaging—all instantaneous ways that we can address urgent concerns with just a click or a tap, all of which are accessible with mobile devices, so we can stay in touch while on the go. Leaders need to use these technological advances to their advantage and be willing to utilize a variety of means for communication so that they can connect with people in the ways that they prefer to be connected with.

Embrace technology

Technology is moving forward with breakneck speed. The advancements in each sector of learning and ability are moving businesses farther ahead with each development. In order for an organization to thrive in the Knowledge Age, it needs leaders who are willing to dive in and become proficient in the use of new technology as it hits the market. Technology is a driving force in the business world today. New technologies are now being developed and implemented at a rate that is exponentially greater than in the past. By staying up to speed with technological advancements, leaders can do their part to help usher their organizations into the 21st century by embracing it themselves. While no one can know everything, good leaders will become familiar with the practices they expect their employees and team members to embrace, and when possible, they will have a working knowledge of such. They will be able to encourage, question, and discuss competently the parts of the whole in regard to their organization.

Be willing to sacrifice for the greater good

A leader cannot reasonably ask for his or her staff members to make sacrifices for the sake of the betterment of the organization without showing that he or she is also willing to make sacrifices. This goes back to leading by example: You cannot reasonably give the executive cabinet their usual holiday bonuses while asking your employees to take pay cuts after a particularly rocky fiscal year. If you want your staff to embrace a change you have proposed, you must also be willing to make some changes of your own.

The times are changing at a rapid pace, and organizations must change along with them, lest they risk succumbing to irrelevance as the world of the modern age passes them by. However, simply tasking staff with changing will not cut it—change has to be modeled by an organization's leadership in order to be effective. When employees feel inspired by a leader who is willing to step up and *be* an example, rather than just *giving* one, they are more open to following suit and embracing change for themselves.

"When we are no longer able to change a situation we are challenged to change ourselves." ~ *Victor E. Frankel*

Chapter 7: Staying Relevant in the Age of Knowledge

"Today, companies have to radically revolution themselves every few years just to stay relevant. That's because technology and the Internet have transformed the business landscape forever. The fast paced digital age has accelerated the need for companies to become agile."
~ *Nolan Bushnell, founder of Atari and Chuck E. Cheese*

If an organization is to maintain its relevance in this bold new era of the Knowledge Age, there must be a shift away from outmoded, traditional ways of conducting business and a shift toward and the adoption of a fresh outlook on how the organization should be run. As discussed previously, change is a major factor in the 21st century, and it affects everyone—from individuals to organizations. Having leaders and staff with the willingness and ability to adapt to change is crucial to an organization maintaining its relevance in the modern age.

In the Knowledge Age, learning is key—and you may be surprised at who the students are: Everyone from a maintenance worker to an executive staff member must get on board the learning train. Intellectual capital is more important than ever—in some ways trumping financial capital. Recognizing this and putting intellectual capital to good use is another vital part of an organization's success in the modern age.

The ways in which we communicate are changing just as quickly as everything else in today's world, in large part due to swift advances in technology. These technological advances enable newer, better, more efficient means of communication that a 21st

century organization needs to utilize if it is to continue to be a major player in the modern era.

Diversity within an organization is another pivotal factor affecting organizational relevance. In a world where globalization is the name of the game, homogeneity cannot lead to organizational success. Rather, taking on team members from a variety of cultural, ethnic, and socioeconomic backgrounds is the best way to enrich your organization's base of skills and knowledge, with unique people bringing their unique experiences to the table. By combining these people (and their wide-ranging backgrounds and skill sets) into one cohesive yet one-of-a-kind team, a synergistic effect is created—one wherein the amalgamated whole of skills and knowledge and experience a diverse organization has access to becomes greater than the sum of its parts.

A few key points to bear in mind with regard to organizational relevance in the 21st century is now explored.

Everyone is a Learner

In order for the skills gap to be bridged, everyone within the organization must be willing to embrace a *lifetime learner* attitude. From clerk to CEO, every team member needs to accept responsibility for learning the skills that will take the organization to the next level. Most people, when adequately motivated, will enjoy the process of learning new and important information that will further their career or make them more valuable to their company. Traditionally, learning was for underlings—training sessions were conducted by managers who possessed knowledge and fed it to their employees on a need-to-know basis as it pertained to performing their job duties. In today's world, managers and leaders cannot behave as though they are immune to the benefits of learning, and learning cannot be limited to what a manager or leader knows or has learned. Rather, everyone within an organization, including (and perhaps especially) management and leadership should champion the idea that learning is for all. This is yet another instance where leaders can lead by example: By showing that they, too, are willing to learn, leadership can connect with staff members by showing them that learning is an *us* thing, not a *you* thing—it is something everyone must do, from manager to maintenance technicians.

The more people within an organization who are open to learning, the more knowledge those people are apt to have—and if knowledge really is power, then the more knowledgeable lifelong learners (who are continuously gaining more knowledge) an organization has on board, the more powerful it can become. At the very least, this approach ensures that your organization's team is filled with people who are enthusiastic about learning, who will also serve to ensure that your organization's relevance will stand the test of time as it meets the demands of transitioning into the 21st century.

Harnessing Intellectual Capital

The 21st century has brought about another shift: that of the value placed on intellectual capital. No longer is the focus exclusively on number crunching and financial wealth; intellectual capital is the new focal point of the modern era. According to author and businessman Thomas Stewart, the intellectual capital of an organization consists of three forms of capital: *human capital* (the value that staff members give to an organization by way of their specific skill sets and areas of expertise), *structural capital* (the processes and procedures within a company that enable employees to do their jobs), and *relational capital* (the network of interpersonal and inter-organizational relationships that a company has, such as customer relations and relations with suppliers). Business strategy and marketing consultant Allen Hovious explored the value of intellectual capital in a recent article he wrote for *The Tennessean*, where he stated, "Intellectual capital is what gives a business its competitive advantage. But all too often, companies overlook it or misunderstand it when, instead, they should be striving to strategically capture it" (2014, para. 6).

It would appear, then, that a 21st century organizational approach would surely be to focus on *all* forms of the business' assets: financial, structural, relational, and human capital. After all, it is the harnessing of intellectual capital that gives rise to tangible, financial capital. An organization is only as strong as the people and processes within it—lacking these, any company would be sure to fall.

Change Will Come—Embrace it and Facilitate it!

In the 21st century, a stagnant organization that refuses to budge from the status quo is, to be blunt, one that is likely to fall before long. In the Knowledge Age, transformation is a must. It is inevitable—if we do not gravitate toward change ourselves, it will find us. There is no avoiding change in a world that is in a constant state of revolution. Rather than dreading these changes, however, we should embrace change. After all, without change, there can be no growth, and growth is advantageous—even necessary—for a company that wishes to stay relevant in the modern age. By cultivating an organizational culture that has a positive view of change rather than a negative one, leaders can take the first step to facilitating change. If change is viewed as a challenge to be met with enthusiasm and curiosity rather than a threat to the beloved and comfortable status quo, it can be turned to an organization's advantage. It is crucial, though, that leaders within an organization lead by example and embrace change themselves before asking their employees to do so. Leaders cannot expect staff to get on board with bidding a fond farewell to the status quo if they themselves are fraught with fear over the concept of change.

Another important aspect of coping with necessary change is facilitating that change. Making transitions easier for team members is a wise maneuver on the part of the leader attempting to instill a positive view of organizational change. One way that this can be accomplished is by opening an ongoing dialogue between leadership and staff regarding any given change that is being instituted—in other words, giving staff the ability to share their feedback regarding the change with their leaders. This again goes back to helping employees to feel like they have a voice, that their concerns are being heard and addressed, and that they are valuable members of the organization's team rather than little fish in a big pond who had better learn to *sink or swim* in the face of necessary change.

Let's explore an example of this concept: If an organization is undergoing a transition in which change is an utter necessity and leaders approach staff with a hardline attitude of "Change is coming—deal with it or get out; you're expendable, and I can find someone who will cope with the change if you are unable to," this creates a sense of fear and resentment on the part of staff, and will likely lead to higher rates of turnover for the organization.

On the other hand, if leaders approach staff in a way that puts their fears at ease by saying, "Change is coming, and we all have to find a way to make it work—please feel free to approach me with your concerns and your ideas about how we can make it easier for you to do your job while we are in the midst of the transition, because I welcome and value your feedback," this shows employees that they are valued, and it helps them to see that there is a sense of "We are all in this together," rather than drawing a line in the sand between leaders and employees.

Communication is Crucial

Communication truly is the crux of the success of any modern organization. Without the ability to communicate—with staff, with clients, with suppliers—an organization has little hope of surviving in the 21st century. The means we use to communicate can be many and varied, particularly in light of recent advances in technology that allow us to be communicative while on the go. Modern technology such as text messaging, instant messaging, and email allow us to be accessible even when we are not in our offices. Thus, ensuring that employees are equipped with the tools they need to communicate effectively is of utmost importance for the organization of today. Many organizations require their staff members to be simultaneously mobile and accessible. In these cases, rather than saying, "We need you to be available, so make it happen!" it is best to provide company-owned mobile devices (i.e., cellular phones, tablets, etc.) to staff members or to institute a *BYOD*, or "bring your own device," policy for mobile work-related communications.

Being adaptable is a characteristic that extends to communication as well. If someone within an organization refuses to use any other means of communication except voice calling on a landline telephone, this can create quite a few problems for an organization looking to stay afloat in the era of utilizing myriad communication methods. Not only can lack of adaptability with regard to means of communication create issues such as time constraints (no firing off an email with a bright idea in the wee hours of the night with someone who is only reachable by phone during traditional office hours!), it can also lead to a communication breakdown. If an issue is being discussed and one participant in the conversation feels that another team member should be *in the loop* of the communication, it is far easier to bring that team member up to speed by emailing him or her with the correspondence up to the current point in time rather than trying to explain it all over the phone. Being adaptable when it comes to methods of communication leaves less room for missed signals and more room for greater understanding across the board.

Technology Changes Rapidly, and We Must Adapt

Fifty years ago, computers took up enough space that they needed to be housed in large rooms dedicated solely to their storage and utilization. Now, that technology which once filled a room can fit in the palm of your hand. Not only that, but today's tiny computers possess exponentially faster processing speeds and vastly greater capabilities than the computers of the 20th century. Within the past decade alone, such great strides have been made in the realm of technological advancement that it feels that almost as soon as a new tech product is released, it becomes obsolete, having been replaced by the next big (or as is often the case in the modern day, small) thing.

With the rate at which technology is improving and advancing, it is necessary for organizations to familiarize themselves with these new technological advances in order to use them for the betterment of the company as a whole. In an era where technology drives business, it is crucial for organizations to foster a culture of being early adapters of technology, lest they find themselves as obsolete as their technology, and meanwhile, competitors who were more adaptable with embracing new technology continue to thrive.

Resist the urge to resist technology. Forty years ago, the idea of a phone being combined with a camera may have seemed absurd or even other-worldly—something out of science fiction rather than a tool that the majority of the developed world would eventually come to use on a daily basis. When faced with a new form of technology, rather than regarding it with skepticism and doubt, ask yourself, "How can I put this to work for the organization?" By taking a flexible and welcoming approach to technological advances, you can help to secure your organization's relevance in a world of rapidly improving-and-expanding technology.

With Diversity Comes Growth

The 21st century brings us an unprecedented opportunity to create a diverse work environment. With the growing popularity of telecommuting and distance working, organizations are now able to utilize the skills of people from all over the globe. No longer is a company hemmed in, bound by geographical lines to *make do* with the best that a single geographic area has to offer. Rather, an organization headquartered in Canada can hire on freelance workers based out of Australia. While a CEO sleeps the night away in Vancouver, a consultant she or he has hired works the day away on the other side of the globe in Sydney.

This amazing round-the-clock accessibility to people who are literally living in every corner of the world is possible due to the new technology now available to us. Every part of the hiring process, from application to interviewing to the hiring itself, can be completed virtually, in an online environment. There is no longer a need to fly out a remotely located potential hire for a face-to-face interview; Skype and Facetime allow hiring managers to get that face-to-face interview by using a webcam and a keyboard, thus saving the expense of airfare and lodging for an interviewee (who may not wind up being hired after all).

By building up your organization's team with members from diverse cultural and socioeconomic backgrounds, you can create and maintain a corporate environment that is dynamic—and a dynamic environment is a thriving environment. People from various demographics bring with them their own unique life experiences and cultural norms. Rather than trying to force new hires into a standardized mold when they join your organization, it is better to ask yourself this: "What distinguishes this person from others? What unique knowledge and experience does he or she bring to the table?" By taking a welcoming approach to diversity, you can support your organization on its path to growth and enable it to branch out in novel ways that may help it to stay ahead of the game—ways that may not have been possible if all team members were forced into a more homogeneous mold and made to *acculturate* to your organization's already defined corporate culture. By encouraging heterogeneity among the members of your organization's team and allowing them to share their distinctive perspectives with your company, you encourage your organization to embrace diversity and use it to its own advantage.

Increased diversity leads to an increased likelihood of innovation. By bringing people with multiple different cultural backgrounds together in one place—people from various cultures, of various ages, with various belief systems—you can facilitate your organization's ability to create and improve a set of truly unique processes and procedures based on input from your eclectic team members.

With the walls in our society coming down all around us through globalization and technological advancement, diversity in the workplace is a given. Anyone not comfortable with it will have to learn to adapt or be left behind because it is and will continue to be a part of our 21st century world and workplace. Diversity in a dynamic work environment looks much like the cultures and societies we all live in: multicultural, multifaceted, and rich with a wide range of talents, gifts, abilities, and needs. The 21st century workplace will be a place where creativity is celebrated through recognition and reward. All types of citizens will be a part of the work culture, and each one will know that their function in the organization serves a purpose. The products and services of the 21st century organization are those that enhance everyday life or create the ideas and technology that will take us into the future and beyond. The diverse workforce looks beyond regulations, formulas, and blueprints and finds the heart of a matter. What does your organization stand for, believe in, and exist for? That is at the heart of the workforce in your 21st century organization. That is your purpose—and the innovation, diversity, technology, and communication skills along with all the rest are the tools you will become adept at using that will make your purpose a reality and your organization a success.

Conclusion

Being an organization in the 21st century is unlike being an organization in any other era preceding it. The 21st century brings with it new challenges and opportunities, the likes of which have never before been seen. All of those challenges must be met with a unique approach in order to be surmounted—the ways of the past will no longer suffice. All of those opportunities come along at lightning speed and, if not seized within the right moment, may slip from your grasp equally fast.

Modern-day organizations must be flexible and adaptable, willing to bend when the winds of change blow—lest they break. They must maintain a corporate spirit that facilitates change and fosters innovation, because change is the only constant in today's world, and innovation is the key to staying afloat in a change-driven era. Technology is one thing that is changing at an almost absurdly fast rate—and with each technological advancement is an organization taking hold of the latest and greatest technology and using that technology to further its business endeavours. Utilizing available technology before it becomes obsolete (which sometimes seems nearly impossible, considering the rate at which technological improvements are made!) is crucial for an organization looking to keep up with the pace of the modern business world.

There is a gap between the necessary skill sets that are vital to the modern-day workplace and the skill sets that today's employees actually have. However, there are also ways that organizations can bridge these gaps in the 21st century, thus readying themselves to be contenders in this day and age—the Knowledge Age. By changing the way in which education is viewed and implemented, such as combining education and technology and taking the *everyone is a learner* approach, organizations can begin to bridge the gap between the skills their employees have and the skills that are necessary for the organization to grow and thrive in the 21st century. Another way for organizations to bridge the skills gap is to revamp hiring practices in such a way as to encourage diversity. Also, the implementation of mentorship programs and leadership seminars can help to bridge the skills gap by creating a channel through which the expectations of employees and leaders alike can be made clear by way of frank and open interaction between the two. Lastly, organizations should consider reviewing and revising job descriptions in an effort to close the skills gap—starting right at the top with leadership.

Leaders in the 21st century must be willing to make sweeping changes to their styles of leadership in order to cultivate a corporate culture that will make their organizations thrive in the Knowledge Age. By utilizing a transformational leadership style—becoming visionaries who are excited about innovating their organizations and are open to leading by example—and encouraging a lateral leadership model where leadership comes from every side, modern-day leaders can be the beacons of hope for their organizations and the life line that keeps those organizations from death by stagnation.

Education, technology, communication, and diversity make up the core of the thriving 21st century organization. These are what every modern business needs to take hold of with gusto in order to maintain relevance in these times of continuous change. By taking a stance that learning is for everyone and is a lifelong process, by embracing technological advancements with open arms and using them to stimulate better, faster means of communication, and by approaching diversity in the workplace as something to be welcomed rather than worried over, organizations in the Knowledge Age can ensure that their legacies live on—in this century and in those to come.

References

Canadian Centre of Occupational Health and Safety. (2012). *Mental health - Psychosocial risk factors in the workplace.* Retrieved from http://www.ccohs.ca/oshanswers/psychosocial/mentalhealth_risk.html

Centers for Disease Control and Prevention. (1996, July). Violence in the workplace [Intelligence Bulletin 57]. Retrieved from http://www.cdc.gov/niosh/docs/96-100/

Cherniss, C., Goleman, D., Emmerling, R., Cowan, K., & Adler, M. (1998). *Bringing emotional intelligence to work.* Retrieved from http://www.eiconsortium.org/pdf/technical_report.pdf

FindLaw. (2014). *Employment discrimination: Overview.* Retrieved from http://employment.findlaw.com/employment-discrimination/employment-discrimination-overview.html

Goleman, D. (2013). *Focus: The hidden driver of excellence.* New York, NY: Harper.

Harris Interactive. (2011, August 11). *Seventy-one percent of employers said they value emotional intelligence in an employee more than IQ.* Retrieved from http://www.careerbuilder.com/share/aboutus/pressreleasesdetail.aspx?id=pr652&sd=8%2f18%2f2011&ed=12%2f31%2f2011

Hovious, A. (2014, September 26). Intellectual capital an undervalued asset. *The Tennessean.* Retrieved from http://www.tennessean.com/story/money/2014/09/27/intellectual-capital-undervalued-asset/16249635/

Occupational Safety and Health Administration of the United States Department of Labour. (2014). Workplace violence. *Health and Safety Topics*. Retrieved from https://www.osha.gov/SLTC/workplaceviolence/

Salovey, P., & Mayer, J. D. (1990). *Emotional intelligence*. Retrieved from http://www.unh.edu/emotional_intelligence/EIAssets/EmotionalIntelligenceProper/EI1990%20Emotional%20Intelligence.pdf

Senge, P. (2006). *The fifth discipline: The art & practice of the learning organization*. New York, NY: Double Day.

Tarkin, L. (2012, September 5). Work hard, play harder: Fun at work boosts creativity, productivity. *FoxNews*. Retrieved from http://www.foxnews.com/health/2012/09/13/work-hard-play-harder-fun-at-work-boosts-creativity-productivity/

Trilling, B., & Fadel, C. (2009). *21st century skills: Learning for life in our times*. San Francisco, CA: Jossey-Bass.

U.S. Equal Employment Opportunity Commission. (2000). *Title VII of the Civil Rights Act of 1964*. Retrieved from http://www.eeoc.gov/laws/statutes/titlevii.cfm

Yang, D. (2013, August 2). Can we fix the skills gap? [Blog message]. Retrieved from http://www.forbes.com/sites/groupthink/2013/08/02/can-we-fix-the-skills-gap/

www.ingramcontent.com/pod-product-compliance
Lightning Source LLC
Chambersburg PA
CBHW051814170526
45167CB00005B/2013